Steinbeck Bibliographies:
An Annotated Guide

by
Robert B. Harmon

The Scarecrow Press, Inc.
Metuchen, N.J., & London
1987

Library of Congress Cataloging-in-Publication Data

Harmon, Robert B. (Robert Bartlett), 1932–
    Steinbeck bibliographies.

    Includes indexes.
    1. Steinbeck, John, 1902–1968--Bibliography.
2. Bibliography--Bibliography--Steinbeck, John,
1902-1968. I. Title.
Z8839.4.H29 1987   016.813'52   86-33830
[PS3537.T3234]
ISBN 0-8108-1963-5

Dedicated to the Memory of

Dr. Robert H. Woodward, 1925-1985,

Steinbeck Scholar and Bibliographer

CONTENTS

PREFACE

For anyone interested in the development of American literature, John Steinbeck presents a most fascinating and intrigu-
ing enigma. On the surface much of his writing has appealed
to a broad spectrum of readers both in the United States and
abroad. Members of the so-called "literary establishment,"
on the other hand, have a tendency to view Steinbeck as a
"flawed artist," who at times demonstrated literary brilliance
but generally created little of genuine merit; they then blithely
consign him to the dustbin of literary history. Even though
his acceptance in literary circles and his image in general
have improved markedly in the two decades since his death,
the controversy over the quality of Steinbeck's writing and
his place in American letters still continues unabated.

When one adds to this controversy the ever-expanding
proliferation of related literature, the real John Steinbeck becomes even more elusive. Sifting through this mass of information for understanding thus becomes a monumental task.
This guide has been designed to make this activity easier and
possibly even enjoyable.

Within the sphere of systematic or enumerative bibliography, the author bibliography is perhaps the most common
or well known. Like all bibliographies of this genre, they
encompass one or even a group of writers and vary widely
in degrees of comprehensiveness. Although there is some
disagreement with regard to definition, a bibliography is basically a systematic list of materials, for a particular purpose,
that share common characteristics. In this instance the main
function of bibliographies is to find out what others have already said or written about John Steinbeck and to identify
what he, himself, wrote during his controversial career.

Among other functions, bibliographies form an indispensable link between those who produce information and

those who consume it. They are, in another sense, analogous to a map or a chart in that they serve as a guide for the user in the chaotic world of literature and other forms of communication. Just as no sensible navigator would set out to sea without a chart, no researcher can hope to find information on John Steinbeck without using such various types of bibliographies as checklists, card catalogs, or indexes. In short, bibliographies exist, if compiled adequately, to bring order out of chaos. By the same token, if they are incomplete or contain erroneous information, they can greatly hinder the search for information.

This guide is organized into three major parts: an introductory chapter, an annotated list of over 200 bibliographic documents arranged alphabetically by main entry, and a series of five indexes keyed to the documents via their sequential numbering system.

Selection of bibliographical documents for this work was based largely on their applicability to Steinbeck studies, hence, the inclusion of major Steinbeck bibliographies of such types as books, periodical articles, and parts of other publications. However, some marginal items are included to provide examples of the diverse nature of many types of source materials where bibliographical information can be located.

I have attempted here to design a guide that will provide the user with greater access to the burgeoning amount of information that is currently being produced about John Steinbeck. I also hope to encourage more bibliographical activities with regard to sparsely covered areas in the vast amount of Steinbeck literature.

In preparing this work I am indebted to many individuals who have encouraged and assisted me in bibliographical work over the years. I am particularly indebted to Dr. Robert J. DeMott, director of the Steinbeck Research Center at San Jose State University, who has been a constant inspiration and source for relevant information. Also, I am grateful to the late Dr. Robert H. Woodward, to whom this work is dedicated, for his devotion to Steinbeck bibliography and his helpful suggestions to some of my previous endeavors. As with all works of this kind, the sins of omission and commission are unavoidable and they are all mine.

Robert B. Harmon
San Jose, California

INTRODUCTION

THE DEVELOPMENT OF STEINBECK BIBLIOGRAPHY:
A BRIEF HISTORY

Bibliographies come in numerous formats and subjects.
In essence they form a great communication network that al-
lows us to locate quickly vast amounts of information. With
the development of electronic databases both the volume and
speed by which we can access needed data have been enhanced manyfold.

Some people recognized early that John Steinbeck would
be a major force in American literature and began to record
his work bibliographically. The first of these pioneers was
Lawrence Clark Powell, who began to collect Steinbeck materials as early as 1934. He compiled a checklist of Steinbeck's
works that was published in the April 19, 1937, issue of Publishers' Weekly (see: No. 151). This was followed by his
article, "Toward a Bibliography of John Steinbeck," which
appeared in the Autumn 1938 issue of The Colophon (see:
No. 152).

The year 1939, when Steinbeck published his monumental work The Grapes of Wrath, saw two other works of bibliographical importance published. Possibly influenced by Powell's article, Lewis Gannett produced his pamphlet John Steinbeck: Personal and Bibliographical Notes (see: No. 63),
which adds some biographical information on Steinbeck to a
list of his works published to that time. Issued almost simul-
taneously was Harry T. Moore's The Novels of John Steinbeck:
A First Critical Study (see: No. 139), which provided a descriptive bibliography of Steinbeck's major works.

From 1939 to 1958 bibliographies attached to various
critical works appeared in a number of unpublished doctoral
dissertations and master's theses. Peter Lisca, in the published version of his doctoral dissertation entitled The Wide

World of John Steinbeck (see: No. 124), included a working
checklist of Steinbeck's publications that also provided a list
of dispatches by Steinbeck from the European War Theater
that appeared in the New York Herald Tribune from June 21
to December 10, 1943, as well as in some other British and
American newspapers. Warren G. French, in his important
study entitled John Steinbeck (1961), included an annotated
bibliography of works by and about Steinbeck. A second
drastically revised edition of this study was published in 1975
(see: No. 62).

In 1963 the Humanities Research Center at the University of Texas at Austin issued a catalog entitled John Steinbeck: An Exhibition of American and Foreign Editions (see:
No. 189). At the time of its publication this work was the
most extensive one of its kind describing 36 Steinbeck titles
as well as listing foreign editions and providing illustrations.
Two important bibliographies covering critical materials were
published during 1965. The first of these, "Criticism of John
Steinbeck: A Selected Checklist," compiled by Maurice Beebe
and Jackson R. Bryer in the Spring issue of Modern Fiction
Studies (see: No. 14), included many items in a classified
arrangement. In the May-August issue of the Bulletin of Bibliography (see: No. 178) is Joan Steele's article, "John Steinbeck: A Checklist of Biographical, Critical, and Bibliographical Material." This bibliography also has a classified arrangement and includes citations of earlier published bibliographies.
Although these two bibliographies contain some duplication,
they actually supplement each other.

Perhaps the singular most important bibliography on
John Steinbeck was published in 1967, compiled by Tetsumaro
Hayashi of Ball State University. This work, entitled John
Steinbeck: A Concise Bibliography (1929-1965), was the most
comprehensive published up to this time in terms of coverage.
Professor Hayashi started compiling his bibliography in 1960
and has provided scholars and researchers with a valuable
tool even though it is a little uneven in spots. Because it
contains some typos which seem to plague most works of this
magnitude, one will find his 1973 and 1983 bibliographies more
desirable.

Another bibliographical milestone in Steinbeck studies
was reached in 1975 with the publication of the Goldstone/Payne
bibliography (see: No. 67) by the Humanities Research Center

at the University of Texas at Austin. This descriptive catalogue of the Adrian H. Goldstone collection has remained the
most authoritative bibliographical source for Steinbeck materials even though it excludes much critical material and does
contain some errors.

    In 1973, Tetsumaro Hayashi published an expanded and
structurally improved version of his 1967 bibliography under
the title, A New Steinbeck Bibliography (1929-1971) (see:
No. 87). A supplementary volume covering the period 1971-
1981 was published in 1983 (see: No. 88). In the past few
years a number of special bibliographies, such as Robert De-
Mott's Steinbeck's Reading (1984; see: Nos. 45 and 46), and
several booksellers' catalogs have provided additional bibliographic information. Apparently other bibliographies are in
various stages of completion covering such areas as critical
materials and Steinbeck editions. Also, new electronic databases carrying Steinbeck-related materials are coming online,
like Wilsonline, which includes the Humanities Index (see:
No. 99).

THE STEINBECK BIBLIOGRAPHIC NETWORK

    Despite all of the bibliographic sources that have cited
materials by and about John Steinbeck, bibliographic control
of this vast literature still faces some difficult problems.
"Bibliographic control" is a term used mostly by bibliographers
to designate the degree to which all of the available references
to a subject have been located and recorded. Steinbeck-
related materials seem to pose a particular set of problems in
that there is a rather wide variety of fugitive items which
have gone undiscovered by bibliographers and which surface
from time to time just when one thinks everything has been
located and listed. This problem is exacerbated by the un-
commonly large number of different types of sources in which
these items appear. Then there is the problem of obtaining
a certain item once one has discovered its existence. Such
large Steinbeck collections, as the ones at the Salinas Public
Library and the Steinbeck Research Center at San Jose State
University, are useful but not always convenient to many researchers who cannot visit such libraries. This is where interlibrary loan arrangements can be valuable. Some Steinbeck-
related materials discovered by means of the bibliographic tools
cited in this bibliography can possibly be obtained by checking

with the interlibrary loan department of your local public or
academic library.

The types of bibliographic sources related to Steinbeck
studies are numerous, but for the purpose of this work
twenty-four types have been defined. These categories are
not mutually exclusive, and some sources can fit into one or
more; however, the sources discussed below are associated
with those categories into which they seem to fit the best.

Abstracting Services

An abstracting service lists and provides digests or
summaries of books, periodical articles, and other literature.
Abstracts may be in the original language in which the item
or items appeared, or they may be translated into English or
another language. A good example is Dissertation Abstracts
International (see: No. 47). See also: Nos. 6, 132, and
176.

Bibliographical Articles

Researchers often overlook periodicals as sources of
bibliographic information. Often they provide excellent
bibliographic coverage of important authors. John Steinbeck
is well represented by this type of source of which Joan
Steele's "John Steinbeck: A Checklist of Biographical, Critical, and Bibliographical Material" (see: No. 178) is a prime
example. See also: Nos. 14, 17, 42, 46, 73, 78, 79, 81,
82, 86, 89, 94-96, 138, 142, 151-152, 166-168, 170, 172, and
173. Several bibliographical indexes are good sources for
discovering the existence of bibliographical articles, such as
the Bibliographic Index (see: No. 18) and the Humanities
Index (see: No. 99).

Biographical Dictionaries with Bibliography

Biographical dictionaries are normally useful for finding
limited biographical information about authors. Some of these
include discussions of specific literary works, and others
contain lists of critical works about authors. Fred Millett's
Contemporary American Authors (see: No. 134) provides an

excellent example of this type of bibliographic source. See
also: Nos. 113, 114, and 141. These sources are useful
usually for general information and are not meant to be extensive.

Biographical Indexes

Because of the many biographical materials available
today, indexes become increasingly important bibliographical
tools. The Author Biographies Master Index (see: No. 11)
links you to a large number of biographical sources discussing
John Steinbeck. See also: Nos. 19, 75, and 76.

Biographies with Bibliographies

Well-documented biographies can be excellent sources
for bibliographical information. Jackson J. Benson's monumental work, The True Adventures of John Steinbeck, Writer
(see: No. 15), published in 1984, contains a wealth of this
type of data. See also: Nos. 63 and 109a.

Booksellers' Catalogs

Over the years the catalogs of booksellers have been
a major source of bibliographical information including primary and secondary Steinbeck materials. In recent years
several have been entirely devoted to Steinbeck. Bradford
Morrow's catalog John Steinbeck: A Collection of Books and
Manuscripts Formed by Harry Valentine of Pacific Grove,
California (see: No. 140) is a prime example. Some of these
catalogs contain much additional descriptive information of
value to Steinbeck scholars. See also: Nos. 16a, 49a, and
136.

Citation Indexes

Citation indexes are useful not only for locating critical
materials about John Steinbeck but for finding others who are
working in specific areas of Steinbeck studies. The Arts and
Humanities Citation Index (see: No. 8) and its online equiva-
lent are extensive sources for periodical materials largely
because of their international scope. See also: No. 175.

Critical Studies with Bibliography

This category contains the most entries of the group discussed here. Some of these do not include bibliographies per se but do contain documentation in the form of footnotes, which makes them useful for finding Steinbeck-related information. Peter Lisca's The Wide World of John Steinbeck (see: No. 124) is a good example of a critical Steinbeck study containing a useful selected bibliography. See also: Nos. 5, 9, 10, 26, 27, 39, 40, 48, 49, 49b, 54, 60-62, 64, 68, 70, 92, 93, 103, 104, 107, 119, 123, 126, 130, 135, 139, 146-148, 154, 157, 161, 163, 171, 180, 184-187, 192, 195, and 201.

Dictionaries with Bibliography

Though an unusual practice, more and more dictionary-type publications are including bibliograhical references. One related to Steinbeck which researchers will find useful is John Steinbeck: A Dictionary of His Fictional Characters (see: No. 84), edited by Tetsumaro Hayashi. This work contains an excellent bibliography.

Dissertations

Due to their diversity of subject matter and the extent of the research involved, doctoral dissertations provide excellent sources for bibliographical information. "A New Eye in the West: Steinbeck's California Fiction," completed at the University of California at Davis by Louis Dean Owens (see: No. 147a), which evolved into a book, John Steinbeck's Re-Vision of America (see: No. 147), is a good example. It is the only one included in this work. One can locate others by using Dissertation Abstracts International (see: No. 47).

Exhibition Catalogs

From time to time catalogs of exhibitions are published to accompany these special events. John Steinbeck: An Exhibition of American and Foreign Editions (see: No. 189), published by the Humanities Research Center at the Univer-

sity of Texas at Austin, contains a great deal of descriptive
bibliographic information useful to Steinbeck specialists and
researchers.

Indexing Services

Included in this category are indexing services that
scan different types of materials to include books, periodicals, and the like. An example is the Bibliographic Index
(see: No. 18). Also these services are published several
times during the year and are usually cumulated annually.
See also: Nos. 20, 21, 37, 51, and 100.

Library Catalogs

During the past decade or so we have witnessed the
issuance of several catalog-type publications covering special
collections located in some academic institutions in the United
States. An excellent example is the recent publication The
Steinbeck Research Center at San Jose State University: A
Descriptive Catalogue (see: No. 200) compiled by the late
Robert H. Woodward. See also: Nos. 67, 91, 162, and 177.

National Bibliography

Thse bibliographies are comprehensive or almost complete records of the printed output in a given country,
furnishing descriptions and supplying verification that cannot
be found in the less complete bibliographies. Since they
sometimes give prices, they have a special use for booksellers
and also are considered as trade bibliographies. The Cumulative Book Index (see: No. 36) is a good example.

Online Databases

Perhaps the most expansive development in the area of
bibliography is the proliferation of machine-readable databases
that include items related to Steinbeck studies. One of the
largest of these is the MLA Bibliography (File 71) in the
DIALOG system (see: No. 137). See also: Nos. 2, 8, 47,
50, 128, 175, and 176. It is expected that these databases
will expand enormously in the future.

Periodical Indexes

It would not be possible to make use of the countless pieces of Steinbeck information in periodicals without the aid of indexes. The function of an index to periodical literature is to point out the location of the topics discussed in the periodicals covered by the index, including John Steinbeck. Here this category includes such general periodical indexes as the Readers' Guide to Periodical Literature (see: No. 156), and the Humanities Index (see: No. 99) covering scholarly articles. See also: Nos. 4, 25, and 128.

Periodicals

Several periodicals directly related to John Steinbeck are currently being published. They contain much bibliographic information of value to Steinbeck researchers. Perhaps the best example is the Steinbeck Quarterly which carries an annual index (see: No. 183). See also: Nos. 105, 181, and 182a.

Steinbeck Bibliographies

Included in this category are those bibliographies of a book or pamphlet nature, dealing only with John Steinbeck, which are not associated with such special events as an exhibition or are catalogs of special collections located in libraries. Such a bibliography is Tetsumaro Hayashi's A New Steinbeck Bibliography (see: Nos. 87 and 88). See also: Nos. 13, 41, 43-45, 71, 72, 77, 80, 83, 85, 91, 121, and 182.

Steinbeck Works with Bibliography

Some Steinbeck editions have been issued with a bibliography appended. For example, Peter Lisca added a bibliography to the Viking Critical Library edition of The Grapes of Wrath, first published in 1972 (see: No. 122). Also, Robert E. Morsberger added a bibliography to the 1975 Viking edition of Viva Zapata! (see: No. 179).

Subject Bibliographies

Subject bibliographies are lists in which both the purpose of compilation and the common characteristics of the listed materials are related to the subject matter of their contents. Such a bibliography with listings related to John Steinbeck is Magill's Bibliography of Literary Criticism by Frank N. Magill (see: No. 129). See also: Nos. 1, 3, 6a, 12, 16, 22, 24, 28, 52, 53, 55, 56, 66, 98, 102, 106, 111, 112, 116-118, 120, 125, 133, 137, 144, 145, 153, 155, 158a, 159, 174, 188, 191, 193, 194, 196b, 198, and 199. There are many other subject bibliographies of a general nature containing references related to John Steinbeck that are not included in this guide.

Subject Indexes

There are several indexes that cover specific subjects, like Patricia P. Havlice's Index to American Author Bibliographies (see: No. 74). These indexes scan many publications that would go undiscovered otherwise. See also: Nos. 2, 7, 29, 30, 31, 101, 110, 150, 164, 165, and 196a.

Theses

Like doctoral dissertations, some master's theses offer valuable sources of bibliographic information for students of Steinbeck studies. Patsy C. Howard's Theses in American Literature (see: No. 98) is an extensive listing up to 1972. A good example of a specific master's thesis is William C. Hilton's "John Steinbeck: An Annotated Bibliography of Criticism, 1936-1963" (see: No. 97) completed at Wayne State University in 1965. See also: Nos. 32, 33, 34, 35, 38, 58, 59, 69, 108, 109, 115, 127, 131, 149, 160, 190, 196, 197, and 202.

Trade Bibliographies

A trade bibliography, like the national bibliography, is a record of printing output in a particular country. It usually lists books in print or for sale. They are used mainly as book selection tools, although their value as a source of

current bibliographical data cannot be ignored. Books in
Print (see: No. 23), as well as Subject Guide to Books in
Print, is possibly the most well known of these types of
bibliographies for Steinbeck-related materials.

Universal Bibliographies

A universal bibliography provides a wide, although
not always complete, survey of the records of a civilization
in many fields and is not limited by time, place, language,
subject, author, or purpose. The National Union Catalog
(see: No. 143) is the most important example of this type
of bibliography providing valuable Steinbeck bibliographical
information.   Others, such as the British Museum Catalog,
are not included in this guide.

*   *   *

In summary, a bibliography may be comprehensive, including all or most of the works of a particular kind.   On
the other hand, it may be selective, containing only a part
of the materials available.   It may be descriptive, having only
a brief descriptive note or annotation; it may be evaluative,
that is, with critical comment; or both descriptive and
evaluative.

As was indicated in the foregoing discussion, bibliographies are found in a wide variety of places to assist researchers in their quest for information on John Steinbeck.
In this quest they locate material on the author; they provide
a means of verifying such identities as names, complete title
of works, place of publication, edition, and number of pages.
If they are annotated, they indicate the scope of the subject
and the manner in which it is treated.   If the annotation is
critical and evaluative, it comments upon the usefulness of
the publication.   Bibliographies point out material, including
parts of books, which cannot be analyzed in other publications; and they group works on Steinbeck according to form,
location, and period.   Dependable bibliographic instruments
remain supremely important for teachers, students, and
scholars.

THE SEARCH AND DISCOVERY OF STEINBECK INFORMATION

In a broad sense the library is a learning center where you may find the information you need for almost any aspect of Steinbeck studies. The problem is to learn how to find what you need, and that's what this guide is all about. There are thousands of good libraries in the United States. There are public library systems, branches of public systems, university and college libraries, junior or community college libraries, libraries within corporations, libraries within museums, libraries in stores, and even libraries in bookmobile units. You can safely assume that there is a library near where you live or work. If you are interested in learning more about John Steinbeck, you should get intimately acquainted with your local library, where great stores of information are available to you. Discussed in the following section are several basic types of material or information you can find in a library that will be useful to you as you use this guide.

Finding Books

Card catalogs simplify the task of finding a particular book among the many volumes shelved in your local library. Here books are listed by author, title, and subject. If you are looking for books by John Steinbeck, you simply look under his name in the author/title section of the catalog. If you are looking for books about Steinbeck, look under his name in the subject section. These catalog cards are usually distinguished by Steinbeck's name appearing in full capital letters at the top of the card (e.g., STEINBECK, JOHN, 1902-1968). You should also notice that various subheadings make it easier to find specific topics. Below are examples of the basic types of subject headings, filed in the order in which they would be found in the card catalog:

STEINBECK, JOHN, 1902-1968. (without any subdivision)

STEINBECK, JOHN, 1902-1968--BIOGRAPHY--YOUTH (subdivision by subtopic and time period)

STEINBECK, JOHN, 1902-1968--CRITICISM AND INTERPRETATION (subdivision by subtopic)

STEINBECK, JOHN, 1902-1968--DICTIONARIES, IN-
    DEXES, ETC. (subdivision by type of book)

STEINBECK, JOHN, 1902-1968. THE GRAPES OF
    WRATH (subdivision without a dash representing a
    specific literary work)

STEINBECK, JOHN, 1902-1968--HOMES AND HAUNTS--
    CALIFORNIA--MONTEREY (subdivisions by subtopic
    and place)

If you already know some of the books dealing with
John Steinbeck, look them up simply by author. At the bottom of each card are the subject headings used for that book.
You can look under these subject headings in the subject
section of the card catalog to find other books on the same
topic. Another way to find books about John Steinbeck is
to consult a bibliography on him. Thse can be located in
the subject section of the card catalog by looking under
STEINBECK, JOHN, 1902-1968--BIBLIOGRAPHY. Encyclope-
dia articles often conclude with bibliographies listing some of
the important books on Steinbeck. Also, a reference librarian
can give you more information about locating and using bibliographies.

In using the card catalog of a library, you can learn
quite a lot about a book and its contents from a card. For
example, the card on page 13 indicates that this book has
illustrations and a bibliography that might lead you to other
materials. The subject headings at the bottom of the card
tells you that the book is primarily a biography of Steinbeck
as a major American novelist in the twentieth century.

Finding Articles in Periodicals

Many articles on numerous topics are published in magazines and journals each year. They are an important source
for information. Often they include information that cannot
be found in books--particularly about very recent events,
very specialized subjects, or particular aspects of a subject.
Since periodical articles are usually short, you can glean the
information you need quickly. Periodical articles on John
Steinbeck can be found by using one or more of the periodical indexes listed in this guide.

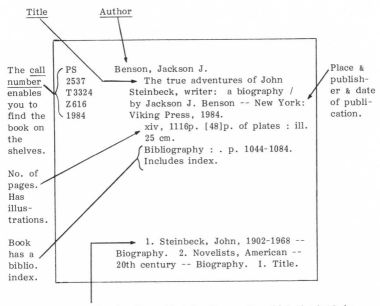

The arabic numerals give the subject heading under which the book is listed in the card catalog. As was stated previously, you may find more books on the same topics, if you look under these headings.

Most students are familiar with the Readers' Guide to Periodical Literature (See: No. 156), a general index listing articles of a journalistic or popular nature. For periodical articles on the more scholarly or critical level, you can consult the Humanities Index (see: No. 99) or the MLA Bibliography. The majority of periodical indexes follow the same general format. Articles are listed alphabetically by subject. Since John Steinbeck is treated as a subject by these indexes, you simply look under his name. Each entry includes the title of the article, the author's name, title of the periodical, volume, page, and date. For example:

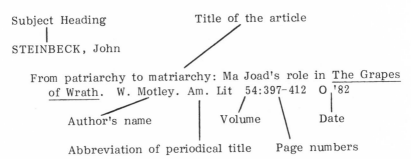

In order to save space, much of the information in the entries is abbreviated. Look in the front of the index volume
at the "Abbreviations of Periodicals Indexed" to find the
full title of the periodical you want. Finding the full title
is very important for actually locating the publication because in most cases the library will have some sort of
periodical list arranged by title. This is also how periodicals are listed in the card catalog.

   You can find information on Steinbeck by checking
such newspaper indexes as the New York Times Index (see:
No. 144a). Throughout his life, and even since his death,
newspaper articles have treated various aspects of Steinbeck's
life and career. Unfortunately, a large percentage of these
have gone unrecorded. Several unpublished master's research
papers cited in this guide (e.g., Nos. 108 and 202) are helpful but cover only a small portion of the total output in this
area.

Finding Biographical Materials

   Up to about 1975 most biographical information about
John Steinbeck was widely dispersed among critical works,
some articles, and a variety of biographical dictionaries.
Since that year, several biographies, including the authorized
biography by Professor Jackson J. Benson, have been published. To find these works in the library, look in the subject section of the card catalog under STEINBECK. JOHN,
1902-1968--BIOGRAPHY. Listed and annotated here are several index-type publications, like the Biography and Genealogy Master Index (see: No. 19), which will assist you in
finding biographical information in various publications.

Finding Book Reviews

   In general, a book review can serve many purposes.
It may help you decide whether or not you want to read a
particular book. For example, if you have trouble deciding
which major Steinbeck biography to read, Kiernan or Benson,
book reviews may help you decide. A book review may include a summary of the subject of the book, discussion of its
style, and comparison with other books on the same subject.
The special indexes discussed in this guide will help you

locate book reviews published in periodicals. To find a review in one of these indexes, you should know:

> the author's name,

> the title of the book, and

> the year that the book was originally published.

The year is most important because reviews usually appear
soon after the book is published, and because most indexes
arrange reviews by year. However, if you do not find a
review in the index covering the date of publication, scan
the index one or two years following since some reviews do
appear late.

Finding Literary Criticism

This guide will help you find critiques of Steinbeck's
work in general, as well as on his short stories, novels, and
other publications. Since it is not always possible to find
criticism of a particular short story, you may have to look
for general criticism of Steinbeck's work and apply what you
read to the short story you are studying. However, some
bibliographical tools, like Twentieth-Century Short Story
Explication by Warren S. Walker (see: Nos. 193-194), will
help you find criticisms on most short stories. Critical
studies on Steinbeck novels and nonfiction can be located
under such subject headings in the card catalog as STEIN-
BECK, JOHN, 1902-1968--CRITICISM AND INTERPRETATION,
for general studies, or STEINBECK, JOHN, 1902-1968. OF
MICE AND MEN. for criticism of a specific work. Always
keep in mind that if you have trouble finding criticism on
any aspect of Steinbeck studies, ask a reference librarian
for suggestions of additional sources. You will find them
willing to assist you in satisfying your information needs.

THE ANNOTATED GUIDE

Cited below are more than 200 documents representing bibliographic instruments related in some way to Steinbeck studies.
They are arranged alphabetically by main entry (either by
author, title, or corporate body), and each item is assigned
a sequential number. Those with lower case letters (e.g.,
No. 196a) were added after the main indexing was completed.
Full bibliographical data are provided, along with an annotation describing the document, its structure, and how it can
be used to find information about John Steinbeck. The annotations are largely descriptive in nature, although some
evaluative comments are selectively included where appropriate. Listed below the annotations are the major subject or
subjects covered by the documents as they are included in
the Subject Index. If a particular work is available online
(i.e., as a machine-readable database), there is a statement
about its availability.

*   *   *

1. Adelman, Irving. The Contemporary Novel: A Checklist
of Critical Literature on the British and American Novel Since
1945. [With Rita Dworkin] Metuchen, N.J.: Scarecrow Press,
1977. 614p.
   Checklists of critical material on many American and
British writers since 1945 are covered in this work. Critical works about Steinbeck are listed on pages 485 to 501.
The first section is an alphabetical checklist of critical
books, essays, and dissertations. The greater part of
this bibliography consists of checklists of critical books
and essays under each Steinbeck title, arranged alphabetically. The third and final section is a checklist of
eight bibliographies.

1. Bibliographies. 2. Criticism and Interpretation.

2. America: History and Life. Santa Barbara, Cal.: ABC-
Clio Information Services, Inc., 1964- . V. 1- .
    Basically this work is an indexing service listing ma-
terials selected from many U.S. and foreign periodicals
relating to political, diplomatic, economic, cultural, social,
and intellectual history in the humanities and social sciences. In 1974 it expanded into a four-part service with
the following subdivisions: Part A, Article Abstracts and
Citations (formerly the one-part America: History and
Life), published three times each year, lists abstracts and
short bibliographic entries alphabetically by author in five
subjects, geographical, and chronological sections, and in
a sixth section for bibliographical, archival, and other
study material. Each issue includes an author index and
a subject profile index (ABC-SPIndex) containing biographical, subject, and geographical descriptors, which are ro-
tated and repeated under each term; Part B, Index to
Book Reviews, is published semiannually and cites, alphabetically by book author, books reviewed from more than
150 key periodicals and reviewing services; Part C, the
annual American History Bibliography (Books, Articles,
and Dissertations), contains all articles from Part A, and
previously uncited book entries from Part B, plus doctoral dissertations. Entries are arranged alphabetically
by author as in Part A; Part D, the annual American History Index, indexes every entry from that volume's other
three parts. It includes an author index and a subject
profile index (ABC-SPIndex). To find materials relating
to John Steinbeck, look under his name in part D. Online Version: Available on the DIALOG System (File 38)
is the database of America: History and Life from 1964
to the present. There are a number of materials relating
to John Steinbeck found here that would be difficult to
find elsewhere. This database is updated three times a
year.

    1. Biography. 2. History and Criticism--Indexes.

3. American Book Prices Current, A Record of Literary
Properties Sold at Auction in England, the United States and
Canada. New York: American Book Prices Current, 1895-
V. 1- .
    Book collectors and others are always interested in es-
tablishing the value of various Steinbeck editions. This

is one of the best sources for this type of information and
includes such items as autographs and manuscripts as well
as printed materials of all periods and in all languages.
Over the years, arrangement and information provided has
varied but generally has included author, title, edition,
place and date of publication, size, binding condition,
where sold, date of sale, catalog number of lot, and price.
To find information, simply look in each volume under
Steinbeck's name.

1. Books--Prices. 2. Manuscripts--Prices.

4. The American Humanities Index. Troy, N.Y.: Whitson
Publishers, 1976- . V. 1- .
     This author and subject index includes articles from
periodicals, newspapers, and other serial publications in
the humanities and related fields. Although the preface
states that "most of these serials are not indexed elsewhere," it has been found that up to 40 percent are dup-
licated in the MLA International Bibliography. Coverage
extends from 1975 forward only. The index is issued
quarterly and cumulated annually. Critical and interpretative articles about Steinbeck are found under his name
in the subject section of each issue or volume.

1. Criticism and Interpretation--Indexes.

5. American Literary Scholarship Annual. Durham, N.C.:
Duke University Press, 1963- .
     Serving as an annual, selective running commentary
on American literary scholarship, this work includes books,
articles, and dissertations. It is arranged as a series of
essays that treat individual authors as well as broader
topics. There is an index of authors and scholars for
each volume in the series. For critical materials on Steinbeck, consult the index of each volume.

1. Criticism and Interpretation.

6. American Literature Abstracts: A Review of Current
Scholarship in the Field of American Literature. San Jose,
Cal.: American Literature Abstracts, 1967-1972. V. 1-5.

Abstracts of interpretative articles were carried in
this publication from December 1967 to June 1972, when
it apparently ceased publication. During its publication
life, this abstracting service was issued semiannually.
The abstracts of articles are arranged under four literary periods and, within each period, alphabetically by
author. The article abstracts are followed by a "Book
Review Consensus," which provides a survey of reviewer-
ers' opinions of selected recent books on topics in American literature. The abstracts of articles about John
Steinbeck appear in the following issues: Vol. I, No. 1
(December 1967), p. 106 and Vol. I, No. 2 (June 1968),
pp. 287-288; Vol. II, No. 1 (December 1968), p. 148;
Vol. III, No. 1 (December 1969), pp. 67-68 and Vol. III,
No. 2 (June 1970), pp. 137-138; Vol. IV, No. 1 (December 1970), p. 53 and Vol. IV, No. 2 (June 1971), p.
112; and Vol. V, No. 1 (December 1971), p. 154.

1. Criticism and interpretation--Abstracts.

6a. Annual Bibliography of English Language and Literature.
London, England: Modern Humanities Research Association,
1921- . V. 1- .
Often referred to as the MHRA Bibliography, this annual publication is an extremely valuable bibliographical
tool that surveys literature from the Old English period
up to and including the twentieth century. Although it
indexes mainly magazines and journals, it does list some
books as well. There is a section on American literature.
The language section is arranged according to subject and
the literature section is arranged chronologically. There
is also a name index. This is a good source for British
materials on Steinbeck. Look under his name in the section covering the twentieth century for citations to critical works.

1. Criticism and Interpretation.

7. Annual Magazine Subject Index.... Boston: F. W.
Faxon, 1908-1952. V. 1-43.
Published in two parts, this rather complicated work
was also combined into a single yearly volume. Part I,
the Subject Index portion, had only one citation of an

article about Steinbeck, appearing in the volume for 1939,
p. 257. Most of the citations about Steinbeck relate to
those works produced as plays. These appeared in Part
II, The Dramatic Index, in the following sequence:
(1938), pp. 191, 247; (1939), pp. 123, 198, 216, 277-
278; (1940), pp. 113, 198, 249; (1941), p. 104; (1942),
pp. 144, 199; (1943), pp. 94, 151, 207; (1944), pp. 131,
151, 212; (1945), pp. 142, 162; (1946), pp. 168, 204,
247; (1947), p. 317; (1948), pp. 257, 276, 313-314; and
(1949), pp. 195, 289, 329. The Dramatic Index also has
an appendix, with individual pagination, entitled Dramatic Books and Plays (in English). Citations relating to
Steinbeck appeared in the following volumes: (1943),
p. 53; (1944), p. 50; and (1945), pp. 20, 38.

1. Adaptations--Indexes. 2. Plays--Indexes.

8. Arts and Humanities Citation Index. Philadelphia: Institute of Scientific Information, 1976- . V. 1- .
    As an access medium to published materials, the cita-
tion index is a fairly recent development in indexing (except in the field of law, where it has been common for
years). A citation index enables the researcher to find
highly relevant materials on a topic by starting with a
piece of research already known, as well as by subject
or keywords. This index is published three times per
year and cumulated annually. Each issue and annual cumulation consists of three major parts: 1) the Source
Index, which lists alphabetically by author the articles
published during the period covered, with full bibliographical citations; 2) the Citation Index, which lists
previously referred to (or cited) materials by the articles listed in the Source Index. This includes items
directly or implicitly cited in the article (works referred
to and discussed, but not formally cited). This section
is arranged alphabetically by the names of the authors
and others cited. Under each cited item is a list of articles and reviews that cited the item during the period
covered; 3) the Permuterm Subject Index, which is an
alphabetical subject index to the materials listed in the
Source Index. Every significant word in the title is
listed. Also, vague or noninformative titles are clarified
by the inclusion of more definitive terms. Under each
significant word, other significant words that appeared

together within that word in a title or additional words
are listed. Following each permuterm entry, the names
of authors who used the word combination in the titles
of their articles are provided. Reviews are given in the
Source Index under the reviewer's name, and in the
Citation Index under the name of the author of the item
being reviewed. Letter codes designate reviews in both
indexes. Significant words in the title of the work reviewed are listed in the Permuterm Subject Index. If
you know of a study related to John Steinbeck and want
to know who is working in the same areas or what is
being written on it, look up this study in the Citation
Index of the appropriate year. Mostly, however, you
will be looking under Steinbeck in the Permuterm Subject
Index to find materials. Because of its extensive nature
and international scope, this index is an excellent place
to locate critical materials on John Steinbeck and his
work. Online Version: Arts and Humanities SEARCH is
available on the BRS system. It includes documents
since 1981, covering articles, book reviews, letters,
notes, bibliographies, fiction, poetry, and performance
reviews of films, theatrical productions, and music. The
coverage of this database is very extensive.

1. Criticism and Interpretation--Citation Indexes.

9.   Astro, Richard. Edward F. Ricketts. Boise, Idaho:
Boise State University, 1976.   48p. (Boise State University
Western Writers Series, No. 21).
        Astro, in this brief study, explores the writings of
Ed Ricketts on their own merits, not particularly as they
relate to John Steinbeck. The selected bibliography on
pages 45 to 48 is divided into primary and secondary
sources.

1. Ricketts, Edward Flanders, 1896-1948.

10.   Astro, Richard. John Steinbeck and Edward F. Ricketts:
The Shaping of a Novelist. Minneapolis, Minn.: University of
Minnesota Press, 1973.   259p.
        Astro provides an analysis of the influence of
Ricketts's philosophy on the writing of John Steinbeck.
Of a bibliographical nature are the "Notes" contained on

pages 233 to 249, arranged in order of their use in the
text of this study.

1. Biography.   2. History and Criticism.   3. Ricketts,
Edward Flanders, 1896-1948.

11. Author Biographies Master Index: A Consolidated Index
to More Than 658,000 Biographical Sketches Concerning Authors Living and Dead as They Appear in a Section of the
Principal Biographical Dictionaries Devoted to Authors, Poets,
Journalists, and Other Literary Figures. 2nd ed. Edited by
Barbara McNeil and Miranda C. Herbert. Detroit: Gale Research Company, 1984. 2v., 1597p. (Gale Biographical
Index Series, No. 3).
     Biographies of major literary figures are indexed in
this set, plus those of minor authors about whom it is
often difficult to find information. Authors are listed
alphabetically by surname. After each name is one or
more abbreviations for biographical works in which the
author appears. To obtain the full title, consult the
key to these abbreviations listed in Volume I or on the
inside cover and fly leaf of each volume. Steinbeck is
listed on page 1357 of Volume 2.

1. Biography--Indexes.

12. Baird, Newton D. An Annotated Bibliography of California Fiction, 1664-1970. [With Robert Greenwood] George-
town, CA.: Talisman Literary Research, 1971. 521p.
     The books cited in this work cover fiction set in
California, not just fiction by Californians. There are
2,711 entries along with indexes of locations and subjects. Twelve major Steinbeck works are arranged alphabetically by title on pages 425 to 428, items 2331 to
2342. Each entry includes full bibliographical data, an
annotation, and a short list of reviews.

1. Bibliography.   2. Book Reviews.

13. Barker, David. John Steinbeck: A Checklist. Salem,
Ore.: David and Judy Barker, Booksellers, c1984. 40p.
     Bibliographic information for this checklist was ob-

tained mostly from rare book dealers' catalogs, some bibliographies, and from the compiler's personal experience.
The checklist is arranged alphabetically by title and under each title in chronological sequence. Most entries
include pertinent bibliographic information along with
estimated retail prices in various grades. Because of
space limitations, foreign language editions, adaptations,
periodical and anthology appearances, critical works,
biographies, bibliographies, or any other such secondary materials are not included. Even though this work
is far from comprehensive, book collectors and booksellers will find it useful.

1. Bibliography. 2. Book Collecting. 3. First Editions.

14.   Beebe, Maurice. "Criticism of John Steinbeck: A
Selected Checklist." [With Jackson R. Bryer] Modern Fiction
Studies, 11 (Spring 1965), 90-103.
         This extensive list covers both critical books and
articles about Steinbeck and his writings. The body of
this bibliography is divided into two main sections:
Part I consists of general studies dealing with Steinbeck's
life and writing; and Part II lists discussions of individual novels and stories, with an index to the general
studies listed in Part I as well as special studies not
previously listed. Titles of the major works on Steinbeck are capitalized. Books and essays by the same
writer are listed chronologically, but no attempt was
made to list all appearances of the same work, generally
giving priority to books over periodicals. Omissions include foreign criticism, unpublished theses or dissertations, transient reviews, and routine discussions in encyclopedias, handbooks, and histories of literature.
(Description comes largely from the NOTE preceding the
bibliography.)

1. Criticism and Interpretation.

15.   Benson, Jackson J.   The True Adventures of John
Steinbeck, Writer. New York: Viking Press, 1984. 1116p.
         This gigantic work is the official or authorized biog-
raphy of John Steinbeck, written by one who is considered to be a leading authority on Steinbeck's life and

career. On pages 1043 to 1084 are "Notes and Sources." In his explanatory note, Benson explains that
he has "listed (1) interviews, (2) unpublished material by Steinbeck ... (3) published material by Steinbeck, (4) published or unpublished material by others
(about Steinbeck or in some way related to him), (5)
notes (listed by page number and key phrase from the
text). Sections (2) through (4) can be considered a
running bibliography of sources, primary and secondary."

1. Bibliography. 2. Biography.

16. Besterman, Theodore. A World Bibliography of Bibliographies and of Bibliographical Catalogues, Calendars, Abstracts, Digests, Indexes, and the Like. Lausanne, Switzer-
land; Societas Bibliographica, 1965-1966. 5v.
        As an international bibliography this work is arranged
by subject with subdivisions per country. Volume five
provides a separate index to authors, serial titles, ano-
nymous works, library catalogs, and like subjects.
Since there is only one bibliography relating to John
Steinbeck, appearing on page 5906 of Volume IV, you
will find this set of limited use.

1. Bibliographies.

16a. Beyer, Preston C. "John Steinbeck: Brief Checklist."
[With Donald L. Siefker] Steinbeck Quarterly, 7 (Spring
1974), 57-59.
        This randomly arranged checklist covers books and
articles that mention or refer to Steinbeck in some way.
Each of the 22 items are annotated, and pertinent bibliographical information is supplied.

1. Criticism and Interpretation.

17. Beyer, Preston C. (Fine Literary Property). Catalogue
No. 1- . Stratford, Conn.: Preston C. Beyer, [197?-].
        Bookseller's catalogs can be excellent sources for
bibliographic information on Steinbeck editions and related materials. Mr. Beyer is a noted Steinbeck special-

ist bookseller, and his catalogs frequently contain items
of great interest to book collectors and scholars.

1. Bibliography. 2. Book Collecting. 3. Catalogs,
Booksellers'. 4. First Editions.

18. Bibliographic Index: A Cumulative Bibliography of
Bibliographies. New York: H. W. Wilson Co., 1937-
V. 1- .
       Many bibliographies separately published or included
in other works are covered in this work which is published in April and August and cumulated in December
of each year. It includes bibliographies published
separately, as parts of books and periodicals. Arrangement is alphabetical by subject, with extensive cross-
referencing. Since individual authors are treated as
subjects, to find bibliographic works relating to Steinbeck, look under his name in each issue or volume.
This work is particularly useful for finding bibliographies contained in book-length studies.

1. Bibliographies--Indexes.

19. Biography and Genealogy Master Index: A Consolidated
Index to More Than 3,200,000 Biographical Sketches in Over
350 Current and Retrospective Biographical Dictionaries. 2nd
ed. Edited by Miranda C. Herbert and Barbara McNeil.
Detroit: Gale Research Co., 1980. 8v.
       This work is kept up-to-date by supplements. Per-
sons are listed alphabetically by surname. After each
name is one or more abbreviation for biographical works
in which the individual is treated. One must consult
the key to these abbreviations listed in the front pages
or on the inside cover and fly leaf of each volume to obtain the full title. Steinbeck is treated on page 423 of
Volume 7. In 1985 a cumulated supplement covering the
years 1981 to 1985 was published in six volumes. This
supplement includes some 2,250,000 additional entries,
bringing the total coverage between the two sets to over
5,500,000 citations. Steinbeck is treated in Volume 5 of
the cumulated supplement.

1. Biography--Indexes.

20. <u>Book Review Digest</u>. New York: H. W. Wilson Co.,
1905- . V. 1- .
    Published monthly, except for February and July,
with annual cumulations, this valuable reference work
provides excerpts from book reviews in some periodicals
and citations to all reviews used. Approximately 80
periodicals from various subject fields are scanned for
this index. Separate subject and title indexes are also
provided. To find reviews to books by Steinbeck, look
under his name in each volume. To find reviews of
books about him, look in either the subject or title index.

    1. Book Reviews--Indexes.

21. <u>Book Review Index</u>. Detroit: Gale Research Co.,
1965- . V. 1- .
    Approximately 450 periodicals and newspapers are
scanned for this index. Although frequency has varied,
it is now issued six times per year, with issues two,
four, and six cumulating the preceding issue. It is also
cumulated annually. There are two major sections to each
volume or issue. The "Book Review Index" section lists
books reviewed under the author, and there is a title index section. Even though no review excerpts are given,
this work is extremely valuable for book reviews related
to Steinbeck because of its extensive coverage of reviewing sources. A master cumulation covering the
years 1969 to 1979 was published in 1980, consisting of
seven volumes. Volumes 1 to 5 list the author entries
while Volumes 6 to 7 list the title entries.

    1. Book Reviews--Indexes.

22. <u>Bookman's Price Index</u>. Detroit: Gale Research Co.,
1964- . V. 1- .
    Listings in this publication are based on descriptions
and prices of books, etc. contained in booksellers' catalogs. Although publication has been somewhat irregular
over the years, it essentially comes out annually. Each
volume includes a list of booksellers represented. Entries are alphabetical by author or title. For materials
on Steinbeck, look under his name in each volume.

1. Books--Prices. 2. Periodicals--Prices. 3. Catalogs,
Booksellers'--Indexes.

23. <u>Books in Print</u>. New York: Bowker, 1948- . V. 1- .
For locating information on Steinbeck titles currently
in print, as well as original prices, this trade bibliography is an invaluable source. Now issued in three parts:
author/title/subject. A list of publishers' addresses is
located at the end of the third part of the title volume.
See also <u>Subject Guide to Books in Print</u>, under "Steinbeck."

1. Bibliography. 2. Books--Prices.

24. Bowker (R. R.) Company. New York. <u>Biographical</u>
<u>Books, 1950-1980</u>. New York: Bowker, 1980. 1557p.
This bibliography is a comprehensive compilation of
information on biographical and autobiographical works
published in the United States since 1950. The
<u>Name/Subject Index</u>, arranged by main entry within
headings for personal names and subjects, contains a
full entry for each title. There are several other types
of indexes contained within this work. Pages 1113 to
1114 list ten titles that carry biographical material
about John Steinbeck.

1. Biography.

25. <u>British Humanities Index</u>. London, England: Library
Association, 1962- . V. 1- . (Formerly: <u>Subject Index</u>
<u>to Periodicals, 1915-1962</u>)
Published quarterly with annual cumulations, this
index scans about 300 British journals in the humanities
and social sciences. It is arranged as a subject index
followed by an author index. Since 1939 there have
been relatively few articles about Steinbeck listed in
this publication. It is, however, an excellent source
for British critical opinion on Steinbeck and his times.

1. Criticism and Interpretation--Great Britain--Indexes.

26.   Burrows, Michael.   John Steinbeck and His Films.   St.
Austell, England: Primstyle Ltd., 1970.   36p.
     Burrows provides a series of comments gathered from
many sources on film adaptations of Steinbeck's works.
Included are many still photographs from these films.
A brief checklist and filmography is found on page 32.

     1. Film Adaptations.

27.   Callow, James T.   Guide to American Literature from
Emily Dickinson to the Present.   [With Robert J. Reilly] New
York: Barnes and Noble, 1977.   272p.
     This work is a general survey of American literature
since Emily Dickinson.   On pages 138 to 141 there is a
brief biographical sketch of Steinbeck's life and a critical survey of his major works.   On pages 248 to 250
there is a bibliography of texts and studies with brief
commentary.

     1. Biography.   2. Criticism and Interpretation.

28.   Chicorel, Marietta, ed.   Chicorel Index to Literary Criticism in Books, U.S.A., Canada.   New York: Chicorel Library Publishing Corp., 1978.   350p.   (Chicorel Index Series;
v. 23).
     The purpose of this work is to bring together in one
place the critical literature that deals with the creative
writers in America and Canada.   Listed here are some
2,448 volumes that contain criticism of 335 American and
Canadian writers.   Organizationally there are four sections in this work.   The first lists books of criticism
alphabetically by critic, providing bibliographic data
and prices for each.   The second section is arranged
by the author under consideration.   Under each author's
name is a number of books about him or her and another
list covering individual works.   Materials are arranged
by region and chronological era in the third section.
The last section lists materials by subject.   Steinbeck
is treated on pages 128, 235-236, and 282.   There are
also some works of a bibliographical nature listed in the
reference books part of this final section.

     1. Bibliographies.   2. Criticism and Interpretation--In-
dexes.

29. Combined Retrospective Index to Book Reviews in Scholarly Journals, 1886-1974. Woodbridge, Conn.: A Carrollton
Press Product, published by Research Publications, 1978-1982.
15v.

    Listed here are more than 1.2 million book reviews
published in 472 journals for the period covered. Main
entries are arranged first alphabetically by the name of
the author. Multiple titles by the same author are then
listed alphabetically, and under each title, reviews them-
selves are listed alphabetically by journal code. Separate
index volumes (vols. 12-15) list book titles alphabetically
with cross-references to principal authors' names. Book
reviews for 14 Steinbeck titles are found on page 147 of
Volume 7.

    1. Book Reviews--Indexes.

30. Comprehensive Dissertation Index. Ann Arbor, Mich.:
University Microfilms International, 1973- . V. 1- .

    The initial set included 37 volumes covering the years
1861 to 1972. It is a computer-generated key-word-out-
of-context (KWOC) index to approximately 417,000 doctoral dissertations accepted by over 380 institutions of
higher education in the United States and some foreign
countries. Since 1973, annual supplements have been
published. In 1979 a second cumulative set covering
the years 1973 to 1977 was published in 19 volumes.
This work is compiled from the entries for Dissertations
Abstracts International and from other lists of dissertations accepted and published by the granting institutions. It is arranged alphabetically by subject keywords
(drawn from the titles of the dissertations indexed).
Under each key word, dissertations are listed chronologically. Each entry cites the source of its information
so you should look especially for the volume and page
number of Dissertations Abstracts International (e.g.,
39/11A. p. 6761) if you want to read an abstract. For
dissertations on John Steinbeck, see Volume 30, pages
569 of the initial set and then under his name on the
Social Sciences and Humanities volumes of the supplements and cumulative sets. See also: Dissertations
Abstracts International, No. 47.

    1. Dissertations, Academic--Indexes.

31. Comprehensive Index to English-Language Little Magazines, 1890-1970, series one. Edited by Marion Sader. Mill-
wood, N.Y.: Kraus-Thomson Organization, 1976. 8v.
       This compilation is an index to 100 English-language
little magazines of the period indicated, 59 of which are
partly or wholly American. It attempts to index files of
defunct publications. Current magazines are completely
indexed through 1970, with some 1971 issues included.
Indexing is only by personal name, with designation of
"Works by" and/or "Works about" under each name.
Book reviews are entered under both the author of the
book and the name of the reviewer, with an additional
subject entry if the book is a biography or a critical
work devoted to an individual writer, etc. Each contribution has been classified as to type: article, poem,
excerpt, play, and the like. Works by and about Steinbeck are found in Volume 7, on pages 4315 to 4316.
There are four items by Steinbeck listed. The list of
articles about him is more extensive and is arranged alphabetically by author. See also: No. 101.

       1. Bibliography. 2. Book Reviews--Indexes. 3. Crit-
icism and Interpretation--Periodicals--Indexes.

32. Condit, Larry D. "John Steinbeck: A Checklist of
English language editions and translations." An MA Research
Paper. San Jose, Cal.: Dept. of Librarianship, California
State University, San Jose, May 1973. 106, [107-108]
leaves.
       The intent of this unpublished research paper is to
provide a complete checklist of the various editions of
Steinbeck's works published up to 1972. The checklist
itself is divided into two major sections, each arranged
differently. The first section lists English language
editions of Steinbeck's works. These are arranged by
year of publication, and then alphabetically by title.
There are 330 entries, from 1929 to 1972, entry number
265 having been omitted. Each entry in the checklist,
both in the English language section and in the translation section, have numbers to the right of the entry.
These numbers refer to the source listed in the Bibliography of Sources located at the end of the paper.
There is also a title index to the English language entries, located on leaves 32 to 35. The second section

lists translations of Steinbeck's works. It is arranged
by language, then alphabetically by English title (trans-
literated), and finally by year. The bibliography of
sources appears on unnumbered leaves 107 and 108.

1. Bibliography.   2. Translations.

33. Corlett, Margaret. "John Steinbeck in Salinas: A Subject Index to Articles in the Salinas Newspapers About John
Steinbeck (from February, 1902-April 1974)" An MA Research
Paper. San Jose, Cal.: Dept. of Librarianship, San Jose
State University, August 1974. 28 leaves.
     The author attempts, in this unpublished research
paper, to provide a subject index to articles about John
Steinbeck which have appeared in three Salinas newspapers from his birth in 1902 through April 1974. This
research paper has three major parts. The first is a
subject index to articles dealing with Steinbeck. This
index arranges the citations under the following broad
subjects: 1) Biography; 2) The Writer and His Writings; 3) Awards and Honors; 4) John Steinbeck Memo-
rial; and 5) Steinbeck Country. In order to offer more
precise information and easier access to the desired
article, the author subdivides these subjects further.
For example, the biography section has four subdivisions: (a) Birth; (b) Youth; (c) Adult Life; and (d)
Death. Under each subject heading the articles are in
a chronological arrangement, as they appeared in the
Salinas newspapers. On leaves 23 and 24, there is a
brief bibliography, mostly of critical works and the
Salinas Californian (newspaper). On leaves 26 to 28,
there is an appendix containing a select bibliography of
photographs arranged under such specific subjects as
names, places, works of Steinbeck, etc. The majority
of these selected photographs are of Steinbeck, his
family, friends, and former home.

1. Biography.   2. Criticism and Interpretation.   3.
Photographs.   4. Salinas Californian (newspaper)--In-
dexes.   5. Salinas Daily Index (newspaper)--Indexes.
6. Salinas Index-Journal (newspaper)--Indexes.

34. Cosby, Arlinda Wing. "Steinbeck in Monterey: The

Criticism of <u>Tortilla Flat</u>, <u>Cannery Row</u>, <u>Sweet Thursday</u>,
1935-1972: An Annotated Bibliography." An MA Research
Paper. San Jose, Cal.: Dept. of Librarianship, California
State University, San Jose, August 1973. 85 leaves.

   The author intends, in this unpublished research
paper, to provide a bibliography that will be a useful
study tool for the Steinbeck scholar or student, either
in examining a particular novel or in researching a more
general aspect of Steinbeck's career as a writer. This
bibliography is confined to published criticism specifically related to <u>Tortilla Flat</u>, <u>Cannery Row</u>, and <u>Sweet
Thursday</u> as novels. Annotations are provided for all
English language citations. Criticism published from
1935 to 1972 is included. A bibliographic citation which
refers to more than one of the three novels is listed under each title. Book reviews are listed exclusively under the particular title. These are designated with an
"R." Citations considered by the compiler as "major
critical studies" are noted with an asterisk. The bibliographies of these three novels have the same format.
Each is covered separately, beginning with an introductory analysis. The citations within the bibliographies
are alphabetical by author (or, if the author is unknown,
by title), keyed "TF" (refers to <u>Tortilla Flat</u>), "CR"
(refers to <u>Cannery Row</u>), or "ST" (refers to <u>Sweet
Thursday</u>) and numbered for cross-reference ease. Articles which appear within published collections of
Steinbeck criticism are listed separately by author as
well as referred to in the collected works cited by
editor. Preceding the individual bibliographies is a discussion of Steinbeck's relationship with his critics and
observations of the nature of Steinbeck criticism as a
whole.

1. <u>Cannery Row</u>--Criticism and Interpretation.   2.
<u>Sweet Thursday</u>--Criticism and Interpretation.   3. <u>Tor-
tilla Flat</u>--Criticism and Interpretation.

35.   Craise, Douglas L. "An Annotated Bibliography of
Criticism in Periodicals on John Steinbeck's <u>The Moon Is
Down</u> and <u>Travels with Charley</u>." An MA Research Paper.
San Jose, Cal.: Dept. of Librarianship, California State
University, San Jose, December 1978. 37 leaves.

   The author intends, in this unpublished research

paper, to provide an extensive annotated list of periodical criticism on The Moon Is Down (1942) and Travels
with Charley (1962) appearing in newspapers, magazines,
and scholarly journals. Following a general discussion
of these two works there are two bibliographic chapters
covering these two works. Within these chapters there
is a further subdivision of entries by type of material:
book reviews and articles, film reviews, and play reviews. All types of materials are listed alphabetically
by author. Unsigned reviews and articles are listed alphabetically by title.

1. The Moon Is Down--Criticism and Interpretatoin.
2. The Moon Is Down (moving picture)--Criticism and
Interpretation. 3. The Moon Is Down (play)--Criticism
and Interpretation. 4. Travels with Charley--Criticism
and Interpretation.

36. Cumulative Book Index. New York: H. W. Wilson Co.,
1898- . V. 1- .
     This work constitutes an indispensable record of
American publications from 1898 to date. It is basically
a dictionary catalog listing entries for authors, titles,
and subjects in one alphabet. Full bibliographic information is provided for each title listed as well as prices.
Many British and Canadian editions are listed. Over
the years, CBI has been an excellent tool for identifying
certain Steinbeck editions not listed elsewhere.

1. Bibliography.

37. Current Book Review Citations. New York: H. W.
Wilson Co., 1976-1982. 7v.
     During its short lifetime, this work included book
reviews published in more than 1,200 periodicals, cited
by author and title. Foreign-language books and new
editions of older books, if reviewed, were included. No
subject listings were provided. Apparently this work
ceased publication at the end of 1982. For reviews of
Steinbeck titles look under his name. For reviews of
related materials, you must know the author.

1. Book Reviews--Indexes.

38. Davidson, Alice. "Criticism of John Steinbeck's Of Mice and Men, 1937-1972: An Annotated Bibliography." An MA Research Paper. San Jose, Cal.: Dept. of Librarianship, California State University, San Jose, December 1972. 52 leaves.

This unpublished research paper attempts to provide a comprehensive list of criticism on Of Mice and Men (1935) up to 1971. Also included is criticism on the play as well as the novel. The bibliography has four major sections: criticism of the novel in periodicals; criticism of the novel in books; criticism of the play in periodicals; and criticism of the play in books. All the entries are annotated. Preceding each main section is a discussion of some general trends in criticism, from the earliest reception of the book to later reassessments of Steinbeck's work. There is a general, unannotated, bibliography of sources on leaves 51 and 52.

1. Of Mice and Men--Criticism and Interpretation.
2. Of Mice and Men (play)--Criticism and Interpretation.

39. Davis, Robert Con, ed. The Grapes of Wrath: A Collection of Critical Essays. Englewood Cliffs, N.J.: Prentice-Hall, 1982. 157p.

Here is a volume of critical essays that provides a well-rounded view of the writer and the work that have had a profound impact on so many other writers. A selected bibliography is located on pages 154 to 157. This list is comprised of major commentaries on The Grapes of Wrath, arranged in alphabetical order by author.

1. The Grapes of Wrath--Criticism and Interpretation.

40. Davis, Robert Murray, ed. Steinbeck: A Collection of Critical Essays. Englewood Cliffs, N.J.: Prentice-Hall, 1972. 183p.

This work is a collection of critical essays taken from various sources. Pages 181 to 183 contain a selected bibliography. It is divided into three main sections: The first lists four bibliographies; the second cites ten books about Steinbeck; and the third contains twelve essays of a critical or interpretative nature. Within each section, the entries are arranged alphabetically by author or title. Many of the items are briefly annotated.

1. Bibliography.   2. Criticism and Interpretation.

41. DeMott, Robert J.   "A Bibliography of Books by and About John Steinbeck."   San Jose, Cal.:   Steinbeck Research Center, San Jose State University, 1984-1985.   10 leaves.
    Prepared as a brief guide for students using the Steinbeck Research Center at San Jose State University, this checklist is a good source for the beginning Steinbeck student.   The checklist is arranged into two broad divisions covering primary and secondary sources.   The primary sources are chronologically arranged within the subdivisions of: (a) Fiction; (b) Drama; (c) Film Scripts; (d) Non-Fiction; (e) Correspondence; and (f) Collections.   In each of these sections a "P" indicates Penguin paperback editions and "A" Bantam paperback editions.   The secondary sources are alphabetically arranged within the subdivisions of: (a) Bibliographies; (b) Critical Studies; (c) Collections of Essays; (d) Biographies, Reminiscences, Cultural and Intellectual Background; (e) Journals: Special Steinbeck Issues; and (f) Additional Entries.

1. Bibliographies.   2. Bibliography.   3. Criticism and Interpretation.

42. DeMott, Robert J.   "A Miscellany of Bibliographical Notes."   Steinbeck Quarterly, 3 (Spring 1970), 41-43.
    This group of bibliographical notes was gleaned from the Lawrence Clark Powell collection of Steinbeckiana at Harvard University's Houghton Library.   All these items at the time were apparently not listed in any other bibliographic source.   Bibliographic information is provided along with the notes.

1. Bibliography.

43. DeMott, Robert J.   "A Selected Bibliography on East of Eden."   Athens, Ohio: English Dept., Ohio University, 1981?   3p.

This checklist is organized into four major sections. Section I covers primary sources; Section II lists correspondence; Section III, contemporary reviews; and Section IV, secondary sources. This bibliography was distributed at the Special Steinbeck Festival held in Salinas, California, during June of 1981.

1. East of Eden--Criticism and Interpretation.

44. DeMott, Robert J. "Selected Bibliography on John Steinbeck." Athens, Ohio: English Dept., Ohio University, 1981? 7p.
    This brief bibliography lists materials by and about Steinbeck. Section I lists books by Steinbeck, arranged in chronological order. It is further subdivided into the areas of fiction, plays, filmscripts, nonfiction, correspondence, and collected works. Section II lists materials about Steinbeck, arranged alphabetically by author. It is further subdivided into the areas of bibliographies, reviews of criticism, reference guides, collections of essays, critical books, pamphlets, monographs, short collections of essays, journals (special Steinbeck issues, biography, personality, reminiscences, and landscape). This bibliography was distributed at the Special Steinbeck Festival held in Salinas, California, during June 1981.

1. Bibliographies. 2. Bibliography. 3. Criticism and Interpretation.

45. DeMott, Robert J. Steinbeck's Reading: A Catalogue of Books Owned and Borrowed. New York: Garland Publications, 1984. 239p. (Garland Reference Library of the Humanities, v. 246).
    This work is the first full-length list of books that passed through Steinbeck's hands during his lifetime and sometimes influenced his writing. The 934 items are arranged in alphabetical order by author and annotated with Steinbeck's own comments in many cases, thus making this work of double interest to the Steinbeck collector or scholar. DeMott also furnishes a lengthy, closely analytic introduction, some engaging illustrations, more than 50 pages of notes, and an

authoritative bibliography. Author and title indexes
facilitate the use of this bibliography.

1. Books and Reading. 2. Library--Catalogs. 3.
Sources.

46. DeMott, Robert J. "Steinbeck's Reading, First Supplement." Steinbeck Quarterly, 17, Nos. 3-4 (Summer-Fall
     1984), 97-103.
     Because of Steinbeck's reading habits, it has been
extremely difficult to track down and list those books
he read, referred to, borrowed, or otherwise had
available during his lifetime. DeMott has made a valiant
effort to do this in his published bibliography but has
found it necessary to provide occasional supplements to
correct, amplify, or refine the original list of entries
as well as to add fugitive titles as they turn up. Consequently in this bibliographical essay he includes:
(a) 18 recently discovered titles and books; and (b)
the present locations of 43 books listed in Steinbeck's
Reading (see No. 45) and in this supplement.

1. Books and Reading. 2. Library--Catalogs. 3.
Sources.

47. Dissertation Abstracts International. Ann Arbor, Mich.:
University Microfilms International, 1838-   .
     A monthly compilation that abstracts and indexes doc-
toral dissertations submitted to the publisher by more
than 380 educational institutions, mostly American but
some foreign (since 1938). In a rather "non-user
friendly" arrangement this work is organized by broad
academic discipline rather than by subject. It provides
annual subject and author indexes. Each entry has an
abstract written by the doctoral candidate and includes
title, author, institution, adviser, number of pages, and
ordering information for microfilm or photocopies. Online Version: Dissertation Abstracts Online (File 35) is
the title for the online service available on the DIALOG
system. It permits search by author, title, and subject
for all dissertations written since 1861. See: Comprehensive Dissertation Index, No. 30.

1. Dissertations, Academic--United States--Abstracts.

48. Ditsky, John. Essays on "East of Eden." Muncie, Ind.:
John Steinbeck Society of America, English Dept., Ball State
University, 1977. 53p. (Steinbeck Monograph Series, No.
7).
    This monograph is comprised of three interrelated es-
says that attempt to focus primary attention on East of
Eden that has come under fire from various literary
critics. There is no formal bibliography in this work
but it does have much textual information about this important Steinbeck novel that will be of interest to bibliographers and scholars.

1. East of Eden--Criticism and Interpretation.

49. Donohue, Agnes McNeill, ed. A Casebook on "The
Grapes of Wrath." New York: Crowell, 1968. 306p.
    This is an extensive compendium of criticism by vari-
ous authorities of the novel published by the mid-1960s.
A selected bibliography is found on pages 296 to 299.
Part I lists in chronological order four editions of The
Grapes of Wrath. Part II is a chronological checklist of
Steinbeck's fictional works. Only the original editions,
all of them published by Viking Press, are listed.
Part III lists six bibliographies, and Part IV lists both
books and articles of a critical or interpretative nature.

1. Bibliographies. 2. Bibliography. 3. The Grapes of
Wrath--Criticism and Interpretation.

49a. Dourgarian, James M. Bookman. List No. 1- . Walnut
Creek, Cal.: James M. Dourgarian, [1982-].
    Like Preston C. Beyer (see: No. 17) Mr. Dourgarian
is a Steinbeck specialist bookseller. Since 1982 he has
issued several catalogs which include miscellanies and
occasional lists of Steinbeck materials. These lists include important bibliographic information of use to book
collectors and scholars.

1. Bibliography. 2. Book Collecting. 3. Catalogs,
Booksellers'. 4. First Editions.

49b. Ehrenhaft, George. John Steinbeck's "The Grapes of

Wrath." Woodbury, N.Y.: Barron's Educational Series,
1984. 120p. (Barron's Book Notes, No. 3413-9).
    This publication is a representative example of
what might be considered a study guide to a noted
Steinbeck novel. A number of these have been published on major Steinbeck titles since the middle 1960s.
Most of these include bibliographies. The bibliography
attached to the publication cited above appears on pages
113-114. As a suggestion for further reading, it lists
critical works related to The Grapes of Wrath, several
general critical studies, and a list of Steinbeck's other
major works.

    1. Bibliography. 2. The Grapes of Wrath--History and
Criticism.

50. ERIC. Washington, D.C.: National Institute of Education, 1966- .
    Established by the United States Office of Education
in 1964, the Educational Resources Information Center
(ERIC) disseminates educational research results and
research-related materials acquired through a network of
specialized centers or clearing houses. Considered as
part of this system are two related hard-copy indexing
services. The first of these is the Current Index to
Journals in Education (CIJE). Phoenix, Ariz.: Oryx
Press, 1969- . V. 1- . (publisher varies) It is
issued monthly and provides author, subject, and abstract coverage of the educational periodical journals.
There is also an index under the title of these journals.
A related service is Resources in Education. Washington,
D.C.: National Institute of Education; Supt. of Documents, U.S. Govt. Print. Off. [distributor], 1975- .
This set is published monthly and complements the preceding service by indexing and abstracting the unpublished literature, consisting mainly of conference proceedings, federally funded research reports, and pro-
fessional papers. Needless to say, these two services
are valuable sources for hard-to-find Steinbeck-related
materials. Online Version: ERIC (File 1) is also available through the DIALOG system. The database is updated monthly and is a valuable source for finding Steinbeck-related material that is almost impossible to find
otherwise.

1. Bibliography.   2. History and Criticism--Indexes.

51. Essay and General Literature Index. New York: H. W.
Wilson Co., 1934- . V. 1- .
     This work is an index to books treating more than
one subject--e.g., collections of essays on literature,
or history, or collective biographies and the like. It
is arranged as a single-alphabet subject/author index
which includes some titles. For essays by and about
Steinbeck, look under his name, starting with Volume
Two.

1. Essays--Indexes.

52. Etulain, Richard W.   A Biographical Guide to the Study
of Western American Literature.   Lincoln, Neb.:   University
of Nebraska Press, [1982].   317p.
     Covering some 350 Western writers, this work is a
bibliography of materials found in books, journals, and
dissertations. Materials cited are limited mainly to
criticism of writers born or reared west of the Missis-
sippi. Following sections that list books, anthologies,
general works, and special topics, the major section
lists materials on individual authors. It is arranged
alphabetically by the name of the writer. Two lists
here are of importance to persons interested in John
Steinbeck. The first covers Ed Ricketts, found on
pages 230 and 231, Items 4054 to 4062, and the second,
on Steinbeck himself, is found on pages 253 to 263,
Items 4464 to 4641. In both these sections, the critical
works cited are listed alphabetically by author. Types
of materials covered include books, articles, bibliographies, and dissertations.

1. Bibliographies.   2. Dissertations, Academic.   3. History and Criticism.   4. Ricketts, Edward Flanders,
1896-1948.

53.   Etulain, Richard W.   Western American Literature: A
Bibliography of Interpretative Books and Articles.   Vermillion,
S.D.:   Dakota Press, 1972.   137p.
     Intended as a handy checklist of 2,255 items for stu-

dents interested in Western American literature, this
work includes bibliographies and other reference works,
general monographs, dissertations and articles, and
regional studies. The main section of the bibliography
provides listings under individual authors, including
their works and articles about them. The bibliography
of books and articles about Steinbeck is found on pages
122 to 126. This listing is arranged alphabetically by
author.

1. Criticism and Interpretation.

54. Fensch, Thomas C., ed. Steinbeck and Covici: The
Story of a Friendship. Middlebury, Vt.: Paul S. Eriksson,
1979. 248p.
      This is a collection of letters exchanged between
Steinbeck and his editor, covering the years 1934 to
1964. Fensch includes a bibliography on pages 235 to
238. It contains books by and about Steinbeck in alphabetical order by author and several other sections
listing interviews, letters, and articles.

1. Bibliography. 2. Biography. 3. Correspondence.
4. Covici, Pascal, 1885-1964.

55. Fenster, Valmai Kirkham. Guide to American Literature.
Littleton, Col.: Libraries Unlimited, 1983. 243p.
      Intended as a guide for undergraduate and graduate
students, this work includes material published through
May 1982. It is arranged by broad topics with all entries being annotated. Materials relating to John Steinbeck are included on pages 194 to 196. There are two
major subdivisions in this bibliography. The first lists
primary sources, broken down into the areas of separate
works, collected works and edited texts, and other
source materials. Items in each of these sections are
listed chronologically by publication date. The other
section lists secondary sources broken down into the
areas of biography, criticism, bibliographies, and reference works. Arrangement of entries in each of these
subdivisions appears to be chronological also. There
are some notes and annotations to items listed in this
bibliography. The user will find this bibliography, although brief, a good place to start.

1. Bibliographies.   2. Bibliography.   3. Biography.
4. Criticism and Interpretation.

56.   First Printings of American Authors: Contributions
Toward Descriptive Checklists.   Edited by Matthew J. Bruccoli.   Detroit, Mich.:   Gale Research Co., 1977-1979.   4v.
    Planned as a field guide for scholars, dealers, librar-
ians, researchers, students, and collectors, this work
attempts to identify the first American printings and the
first English printings of books by selected American
authors.   John Steinbeck is included in Volume One,
pages 353 to 357.   The checklist is arranged in chronological order by title.   For each entry, the full bibliographic information is provided along with brief descriptive notes.   Also included are three other brief
checklists, covering collections, selected secondary
works, and two bibliographies.   Some title pages are
reproduced in a small format.

1. Bibliographies.   2. Bibliography.   3. Book Collecting.
4. First Editions.

57.   Fontenrose, Joseph Eddy.   John Steinbeck: An Introduction and Interpretation.   New York: Barnes and Noble,
1963.   150p.
    This work is considered one of the pioneering ac-
counts of mythological influences on the writing of John
Steinbeck.   A "Selected Bibliography" is found on pages
142 to 144.   It is organized into five major sections.
The first covers "Steinbeck's Chief Works," further subdivided into fiction and nonfiction.   The second section
lists plays and filmscripts arranged chronologically.
Section three lists minor works and is further subdivided
into the categories of short stories, separately published,
and nonfiction.   Section four lists two collected works,
and section five, critical and interpretative studies,
further subdivided into the areas of full-length and
brief studies.

1. Bibliography.   2. Criticism and Interpretation.   3.
Film Adaptations--Scripts.

58.   Fowler, Marilyn J.   "John Steinbeck: A Collection and
Bibliography of His Short Works."   An MA Research Paper.
San Jose, Cal.:   Dept. of Librarianship, San Jose State Col-
lege, June, 1972.   35 leaves.

This unpublished research paper was compiled to
provide, in one place, a listing of Steinbeck articles,
essays, and short stories that do not appear in a published collection of his work up to 1971.   Three introductory chapters discuss the problems involved in collecting entries on such a diverse and scattered group of
materials and the development of bibliographic coverage
to the date of completion of this bibliography.   The main
body of this work is contained in the appendix, divided
into two major sections.   The first is a bibliography of
items collected.   Items listed in this section were added
to the Steinbeck Research Center at San Jose State University.   This section is further subdivided into categories covering short stories, nonfiction miscellanies,
articles and essays, verse, letters, and speeches.   The
second section is a bibliography of items not collected.
It is subdivided into categories covering short stories,
nonfiction miscellanies, articles and essays, newspaper
reports, verse and letters.   There is a bibliography of
sources used on leaves 34 and 35.

1. Short Stories.   2. Correspondence.   3. Miscellanies,
Nonfiction.

59.   Frame, Louise L.   "A Bibliography of Critical Writings
On John Steinbeck's East of Eden and The Long Valley."
An MA Research Paper.   San Jose, Cal.:   Dept. of Librarianship, California State University, San Jose, July, 1975.
45 leaves.

Because of Steinbeck's impact upon American letters,
critical materials relating to his work are important to
both students and scholars.   This unpublished research
paper concerns two of Steinbeck's major works: The
Long Valley (1938) and East of Eden (1952).   The list
relating to The Long Valley is preceded by a short chapter providing a brief history of the work.   The bibliography proper is divided into two major sections.   The
first lists primary sources, including editions appearing
in collections, and individual short stories by date of
first publication, and miscellanies.   The second sub-

division is a bibliography of critical works. These are
arranged into categories under articles and essays, discussions in books and monographs, unpublished dissertations, an unpublished master's thesis, and reviews.
The list relating to East of Eden is also introduced by
a brief history. The subdivision under primary sources
lists printed editions and miscellanies. The bibliography
of critical materials covers articles, discussions in books
and monographs, unpublished dissertations, and reviews.
Brief annotations are provided for the critical works in
both major sections. A bibliography of sources used in
compilation of the bibliographies is given on leaves 42
and 45.

1. East of Eden--Criticism and Interpretation. 2. The
Long Valley--Criticism and Interpretation.

60. French, Warren G. A Companion to "The Grapes of
Wrath." New York: Viking Press, 1963. Reprinted by
Augustus M. Kelley Publishers, Clifton, N.J., 1972. 243p.
    This is a collection of essays, appearing in various
sources, that relate to the Depression era in American
history as well as to The Grapes of Wrath directly. A
bibliography is located on pages 229 to 235. It is divided into the same topics as covered in the nine chapters in the book. Each one is in the form of a brief
bibliographic essay.

1. The Grapes of Wrath--Criticism and Interpretation.

61. French, Warren G. Filmguide to "The Grapes of Wrath."
Bloomington, Ind.: Indiana University Press, 1973. 87p.
(Indiana University Press Filmguide Series, FG2).
    This work is a basic guide to the study of the film,
according to French, "as both an autonomous work of
art and an adaptation of the novel." There is a Ford
Filmography on pages 66 to 69 and a bibliography on
pages 69 to 72. The filmography lists the movies John
Ford directed, listed in chronological order. The bibliography is fully annotated and lists materials under
the categories "About John Ford," "About The Grapes
of Wrath," and "Reviews."

1. Ford, John, 1895-1973.   2. The Grapes of Wrath
(Moving-Picture).

62. French, Warren G. John Steinbeck. 2nd revised edition. Boston: Twayne Publishers, 1975. 189p. (Twayne's
United States Authors Series, TUSAS 2).
        In this revised version, the author focuses on the
    consciousness as exemplified in Steinbeck's writing.
    There is a Selected Bibliography on pages 180 to 184.
    It is divided into two main sections. The first is pri-
    mary source material by Steinbeck, listed under the
    categories of fiction and reports. The second section
    is an annotated list of secondary sources. This bib-
    liography is brief but one of the better ones for the
    beginning student.

    1. Bibliography.   2. Criticism and Interpretation.

63.   Gannett, Lewis Stiles. John Steinbeck, Personal and
Bibliographical Notes. New York: Viking Press, 1939. 14p.
        The author, a former book critic for the New York
    Herald Tribune (newspaper), relates his impressions of
    Steinbeck's development as a writer. On the back leaf
    is a bibliography of "Books by John Steinbeck." This
    brief list contains 12 entries arranged in chronological
    order. The first edition, first issue has a frontis-
    piece portrait of Steinbeck attributed erroneously to
    Stjernstrom. The second issue has Stjernstrom blacked
    out and Bo Beskov substituted beneath. The third is-
    sue has the frontispiece attributed to Bo Beskov and a
    letter from Steinbeck reproduced in facsimile and a
    glossy print of the portrait which is in the Goldstone
    Collection. Three hundred copies of the second issue
    were signed by Steinbeck.

    1. Biography.   2. Bibliography.

64.   Garcia, Reloy. Steinbeck and D. H. Lawrence: Fictive
Voices and the Ethical Imperative. Muncie, Ind.: John
Steinbeck Society of America, English Dept., Ball State Uni-
versity, 1972. 36p. (Steinbeck Monograph Series, No. 2).
        In this study the author compares Steinbeck and

Lawrence in their approaches to the ethical imperative
as revealed in their fiction. Of bibliographical significance in this monograph are the footnotes interspersed
at appropriate positions throughout the study.

1. Criticism and Interpretation. 2. Lawrence, David
Herbert, 1885-1930.

65. Gerstenberger, Donna Lorine. The American Novel,
1789-1959: A Checklist of Twentieth-Century Criticism.
[With George Hendrick] Denver: Alan Swallow, 1961. 333p.
This work is a selective checklist of secondary materials including both general studies and commentaries
on individual authors. The materials dealing with individual authors are arranged alphabetically by author,
with the titles of the novels given beneath each author's
name and the critical citation beneath each novel title.
The general materials are arranged by literary period.
Steinbeck is treated on pages 225 to 230. The first
section lists titles alphabetically with critical works
listed alphabetically by author below. There is also a
general section of books and articles about Steinbeck.

1. Criticism and Interpretation.

66. Gerstenberger, Donna Lorine. The American Novel:
A Checklist of Twentieth-Century Criticism on Novels Written
Since 1789; Volume II: Criticism Written 1960-1968. [With
George Hendrick] Chicago: Swallow Press, 1970. 459p.
A continuation of her previous volume, which covered
the period 1789 to 1959. Steinbeck is treated on pages
315 to 319. The arrangement is exactly the same as in
the first volume except there is a section listing nine
bibliographic works.

1. Bibliographies. 2. Criticism and Interpretation.

67. Goldstone, Adrian Homer. John Steinbeck: A Bibli-
ographical Catalogue of the Adrian H. Goldstone Collection.
[With John R. Payne] Austin: Humanities Research Center,
University of Texas at Austin, 1974. 240p.
This bibliography is perhaps the most definitive to

be published covering the works by and about John
Steinbeck to date. The body of this listing is arranged
into seven sections each covering different types of
materials. Since the Goldstone Collection did not include periodical articles about Steinbeck and reviews of
his books, they are not listed. There are 1,227 citations included within this impressive work. It will be
of particular value to the collector, bookseller, or
scholar because of its descriptions and the scope of its
coverage. There is a useful author/title index on pages
231 to 240. Section A describes in detail first as well
as other important editions of Steinbeck's major works.
As an example, entry A12 describes in full detail, according to the rules of descriptive bibliography, the
first edition, first English edition, and the Limited Editions Club edition of The Grapes of Wrath (1939). These
descriptions consist of a transcription of the title page,
collation, contents, binding details with a note about the
dust jacket, and notes which may include the date of
publication, number of copies published, publication
price, record of previous publication, and the like.
   Twenty-eight other selected editions of interest are
listed with less bibliographic detail. Books in this section are arranged in chronological order. This section
is particularly useful for book collectors and booksellers
who need this descriptive information to identify genuine
first editions. Unfortunately this work does not contain
all of the collectible editions that have appeared in other
bibliographies. Section B lists Steinbeck's contributions
to books, including such original contributions as prefaces and introductions and material previously published
elsewhere. These contributions are arranged in chronological order by year, each source listed alphabetically
by author. Each citation indicates the exact Steinbeck
contribution and the pages on which they are found.
Section C lists Steinbeck's contributions to periodicals,
including original and previously published material.
The articles are arranged in chronological order by year
and alphabetically by title within each year. The as-
terisked items were obtained from other sources than the
Goldstone Collection. Section D includes 626 entries of
Steinbeck's works that have been translated into 54
languages. This section is alphabetically arranged by
language, making it necessary to read through the list
to locate all translations of In Dubious Battle, for ex-

ample, or to check the entries on appropriate pages determined by the index. Section E lists stage, motion picture, television, and radio productions of works by Steinbeck. Also provided are casting and production details. The productions listed in this section are arranged chronologically by date of presentation. Section F lists 74 books entirely or partially about Steinbeck, arranged in chronological order. Section G is an appendix that is subdivided into seven parts: Part I is a list of 17 bibliographies or bibliographically related items; Part II lists secondary material about Steinbeck, most of which are bibliographical in nature; Part III lists related items; Part IV lists blurbs; Part V lists study notes; Part VI lists recordings; and Part VII lists miscellaneous items.

1. Bibliographies. 2. Bibliography. 3. Blurbs. 4. Criticism and Interpretation. 5. Ephemera. 6. Film Adaptations. 7. First Editions. 8. Phonorecords. 9. Phonotapes. 10. Plays. 11. Radio Adaptations. 12. Study and Teaching--Outlines, Syllabi, etc. 13. Television Adaptations. 14. Translations.

68. Gray, James. John Steinbeck. Minneapolis: University of Minnesota Press, 1971. 48p. (University of Minnesota Pamphlets on American Writers, No. 94). This same material was reprinted as part of American Writers: A Collection of Literary Biographies. Edited by Leonard Under. New York: Charles Scribner's Sons, 1974. Vol. IV, pp. 49-72.
This brief work is a tribute to Steinbeck's "storytelling skill," which describes him as "a moral ecologist, obsessively concerned with man's spiritual struggle to adjust to his environment." The pamphlet bibliography appears on pages 46 to 48 and the reprint version on pages 71 to 72 of Volume IV. It consists of two main sections. The first lists works by Steinbeck, broken down into novels, collections of short stories, plays, and nonfiction. The second section lists critical studies in book form only. There is a minor difference in these two bibliographies. The University of Minnesota pamphlet includes a listing of 19 current American reprints in the first section, whereas the Scribner's bibliography does not.

1. Bibliography. 2. Criticism and Interpretation.

69. Gunderman, Patricia. "John Steinbeck: A Checklist of
His Short Stories in Collections." An MA Research Paper.
San Jose, Cal.: Dept. of Librarianship, San Jose State University, May 1975. 46 leaves.
    This unpublished research paper attempts to list
Steinbeck's short stories appearing in such materials as
literature textbooks, anthologies, short story collections,
periodicals, newspapers, and the like. In the bibliography, excerpts from nonfiction are excluded, but those
from Steinbeck's fictive works are included and are given
the distinctive titles assigned for publication and an in-
dication of the work from which it is taken. The bibliography is arranged alphabetically by title of the short
story. If the story appears in more than one source,
the entries are arranged chronologically. A special abbreviation is attached to each entry indicating the source
of the information. A bibliography of sources is provided on leaf 46.

    1. Short Stories.

70. A Handbook for Steinbeck Collectors, Librarians, and
Scholars. Edited by Tetsumaro Hayashi. Muncie, Ind.: John
Steinbeck Society of America, English Dept., Ball State University, 1981. 54p. (Steinbeck Monograph Series, No. 11).
    To call this monograph a handbook is a little mis-
leading. It is more a guide, being a collection of essays
related to Steinbeck collecting and library resources or
special collections of Steinbeck materials. All of the information contained here is of bibliographic significance
and will be of immense value to those interested in research as well as collecting.

    1. Bibliography. 2. Book Collecting. 3. Library Re-
sources.

71. Harmon, Robert B. A Collector's Guide to the First
Editions of John Steinbeck. Bradenton, Fla.: Opuscula
Press, 1985. 60p.
    Book collectors always need assistance in identifying
the first editions of a particular author. This handy
guide is designed in a convenient size so that it can be
carried into a bookstore in a shirt or coat pocket or

purse. The main section of the guide is an alphabetically arranged list of 62 Steinbeck collectible first editions.
Detailed descriptions are provided for each title to aid
in the identification process. Also included is a checklist of 26 Steinbeck literary contributions to periodicals.
Additional features include a list of sources, from which
some of the bibliographical information for this guide
was obtained, a chronological list of Steinbeck titles, a
brief biographical sketch, and an introduction. This
guide is an updated and expanded version of the author's
previous work: The First Editions of John Steinbeck
published by Hermes Publications of Los Altos, California in 1978.

1. Bibliographies. 2. Bibliography. 3. Book Collecting.
4. First Editions.

72. Harmon, Robert B. John Steinbeck: Toward a Bibliography of Bibliographies. San Jose, Cal.: Dibco Press,
1973. 8p. (American Authors Bio-Bibliography Series, No.
1).
      This work contains a brief biographical sketch of
Steinbeck, a chronological list of his major works, and
a bibliography of bibliographies. The body of this bibliography is divided into lists of book- and pamphlet-
length bibliographies, bibliographical articles, and works
about Steinbeck which contain bibliographies. It is not
comprehensive in terms of coverage.

1. Bibliographies.

73. Hashiguchi, Yasuo. "Bibliographical Article: Japanese
Translations of Steinbeck's Works (1939-69)." Steinbeck
Quarterly, 3 (Fall 1970), 93-106.
      This bibliographical essay covers only works by
Steinbeck. It is divided into three main sections. Part
I consists of Steinbeck titles arranged in chronological
order. Under each title the Japanese translations (if
any) are listed in order of publication. If there is
more than one translator for a particular edition, their
names do not necessarily come in alphabetical order.
Part II consists of some itemized comments on the list
in the preceding section. Part III consists of some con-

cluding remarks on the use of translations in the study
of Steinbeck in Japan.

1. Bibliography.   2. Translations, Japanese.

74.   Havlice, Patricia Pate.   Index to American Author Bibliographies.   Metuchen, N.J.:   Scarecrow Press, 1971.   204p.
    This is a checklist of author bibliographies published
in periodicals.   Arranged as an alphabetic list of author's
names with the bibliographies listed beneath each name.
Includes an index of compilers.   This work supplements
Nilon (see: No. 145).   On page 154, items 1865 to 1871,
there is a list of bibliographies related to Steinbeck.
This brief list is arranged alphabetically by author.

1. Bibliographies.

75.   Havlice, Patricia Pate.   Index to Literary Biography.
Metuchen, N.J.:   Scarecrow Press, 1975.   2v.
    This work is an index to biographical information on
approximately 68,000 authors appearing in 50 volumes of
collective biography and dictionaries of literature.   Each
person is listed alphabetically by surname.   Following
the name is a brief statement of the person's nationality
and the nature of their literary achievement.   Abbreviations are then given for the biographical works in
which the person appears.   The key to these abbreviations is located in the front of Volume One.   John
Steinbeck is listed in Volume Two on pages 1129-1130.

1. Biography--Indexes.

76.   Havlice, Patricia Pate.   Index to Literary Biography.
First Supplement.   Metuchen, N.J.:   Scarecrow Press, 1983.
2v.
    Approximately 53,000 authors are covered in this
supplement which indexes 57 additional literary dictionaries, encyclopedias, and biographical sources published between 1969 and 1981.   Steinbeck is treated in
Volume Two.

1. Biography--Indexes.

77. Hayashi, Tesumaro. "Annual Steinbeck Bibliography
(1971): A Checklist of Steinbeck Criticism after 1968."
Muncie, Ind.: The John Steinbeck Society of America, Dept.
of English, Ball State University, 1971. 34 leaves.
     This bibliographical checklist is a supplement to
Hayashi's 1967 standard bibliography on Steinbeck and
was mostly incorporated into his updated version published in 1973. The checklist itself has two major sections. The first section covers primary sources, including editions, excerpts, letters, nonfiction miscellanies, short stories and novels, and speeches. The
second major section lists secondary sources, including
books and monographs, articles, discussions in books,
biography including eulogy, book reviews, dissertations,
master's theses, and poems. There are two final sections covering bibliography, broken into a list of annuals, newspapers, and periodicals indexed, and a list
of bibliographies.

1. Bibliography. 2. Criticism and Interpretation.

78. Hayashi, Tetsumaro. "A Brief Survey of John Steinbeck
Bibliographies." Kyushu American Literature, 9 (July 1966),
54-61.
     Professor Hayashi chronicles the publication of Stein-
beck bibliographies up to 1965 in this bibliographical
essay. He also briefly outlines the task of bibliographies
in the development of Steinbeck studies. The chronological checklist on pages 60 and 61 provides full bibliographical data on the works discussed in the body of
this essay.

1. Bibliographies.

79. Hayashi, Tetsumaro. "A Checklist of Steinbeck Criticism After 1965: First Supplement to Tetsumaro Hayashi's
John Steinbeck: A Concise Bibliography (1930-1965)."
Steinbeck Newsletter, 1 (September 1968), 1-9.
     This checklist is organized into the following major
sections: I. Bibliography; II. Primary sources, including
articles and essays by Steinbeck, also excerpts,
speeches, reprints of novels, and short stories; III.
Secondary sources or criticism of Steinbeck's works, in-

cluding unpublished dissertations, articles, discussions
in books and pamphlets; and IV. Book reviews of primary and secondary materials. The Steinbeck Newsletter
became the Steinbeck Quarterly after 1969.

1. Criticism and Interpretation.

80. Hayashi, Tetsumaro. "A Checklist of Steinbeck's Major
Works (1929-1968) and Recent Books on Steinbeck." Muncie,
Ind.: The John Steinbeck Society of America, English Dept.,
Ball State University, 1978. 7 leaves.
    This checklist covers only the major works by and
about Steinbeck published since 1929. Pages 1 to 3 include alphabetical, chronological, and genre checklists.
Pages 4 to 5 include recent books about Steinbeck published between 1971 and 1978. Two additional pages
list materials of this nature published during 1978-1979.

1. Bibliography. 2. Criticism and Interpretation.

81. Hayashi, Tetsumaro. "John Steinbeck: A Checklist of
Movie Reviews." Serif, 7 (June 1970), 18-22.
    Hayashi claims that Steinbeck's popularity can, in
part, be determined by the fact that a substantial number of his writings have been made into motion pictures.
Part I of this checklist covers movies based on Steinbeck's works. Here 12 movie titles arranged in alphabetical order are listed. For each movie, the publication
date of the book is given, along with the company pro-
ducing the movie and the date. Part II lists the movie
reviews for these motion pictures. These are also listed
in alphabetical sequence and the reviews under each of
them alphabetically by the title of the publication carrying the review. For each review all the pertinent bibliographical data is provided.

1. Film Adaptations. 2. Film Reviews.

82. Hayashi, Tetsumaro. "John Steinbeck: A Checklist of
Unpublished Ph.D. Dissertations (1946-1967)." Serif, 5 (December 1968), 30-31.
    This checklist seems to have been compiled to refute

the notion that Steinbeck's work was of little interest to scholars. It is comprised of 12 entries listed by author in alphabetical order. Hayashi points out that at least two of the dissertations listed were later published in book form.

1. Dissertations, Academic--United States.

83. Hayashi, Tetsumaro. John Steinbeck: A Concise Bibliography (1930-65). Metuchen, N.J.: Scarecrow Press, 1967. 164p.

At the time of its publication, this was the most comprehensive bibliography on Steinbeck. The body of the bibliography consists of two parts: Part I lists primary material, and Part II, secondary materials. Included in the listing of primary materials are such things as verse, letters, speeches, recordings, films based on the major works and a "detailed description of manuscript holdings of Steinbeckiana." Along with book reviews and critical essays, the secondary materials include unpublished theses and dissertations, reviews of critical books on Steinbeck, and bibliographies. Except for a few Japanese journals, foreign language editions and criticism are omitted; dates of reprint editions are not always given; and the chronology, which ends with 1964, omits specific dates within the calendar year. As in any bibliography of this magnitude there are some errors. For example, Ben Abramson and Ben Abromson are one and the same bookseller, noted in various places among the "institutional" holdings. There are few annotations.

1. Adaptations. 2. Bibliography. 3. Book Reviews. 4. Correspondence. 5. Criticism and Interpretation. 6. Dissertations, Academic. 7. Film Reviews. 8. Manuscripts. 9. Plays. 10. Poetry. 11. Short Stories. 12. Speeches.

84. Hayashi, Tetsumaro, ed. John Steinbeck: A Dictionary of His Fictional Characters. Metuchen, N.J.: Scarecrow Press, 1976. 222p.

A remarkably versatile artist, John Steinbeck created a variety of memorable fictional characters. This dictionary provides one the opportunity to see all of these

fictional characters, to understand the nature of Steinbeck's characters and characterizations, and to grasp
the way in which these characters differ and yet see
how they are unified by a common bond of humanity.
A selected bibliography appears in Appendix II, pages
213 to 219. Section A deals with Steinbeck's published
works and is divided into an alphabetical checklist,
chronological checklist, and genre checklist. Section B
covers recent books and monographs on Steinbeck
(1971-1976). This section is broken down by books,
monographs, and other items of importance. Section C
is a checklist of recent doctoral dissertations on Steinbeck (1965-1974), arranged chronologically.

1. Bibliography. 2. Biography. 3. Characters. 4.
Criticism and Interpretation. 5. Dissertations, Academic.

85.   Hayashi, Tetsumaro. John Steinbeck: A Guide to the
Doctoral Dissertations, a Collection of Dissertation Abstracts
(1946-1969). Muncie, Ind.: John Steinbeck Society of
America, English Dept., Ball State University, 1971.   32p.
(Steinbeck Monograph Series, No. 1).
        This work is a collection of 16 dissertation abstracts
chronologically arranged. On pages 23 to 26, the compiler presents a combination bibliographical essay and
annotated bibliography of recent Steinbeck studies published in the United States. There are three indexes:
chronological, subject, and by educational institution.

1. Dissertations, Academic.

86.   Hayashi, Tetsumaro. "John Steinbeck's British Publications." [With Roy S. Simmonds] Steinbeck Quarterly, 8
(Summer-Fall 1975), 79-89.
        The introduction to this bibliography was written by
Dr. Hayashi. The annotated checklist of the British
appearances of Steinbeck's work was compiled by Mr.
Simmonds. It is arranged in chronological order and
is divided into two parts. Part A lists 58 short stories,
excerpts, and essays. Part B lists six book-length
works. The conclusion was also written by Dr. Hayashi.
This article strongly indicates many areas of possible
bibliographical research.

1. Bibliography--Great Britain.

87. Hayashi, Tetsumaro. A New Steinbeck Bibliography,
1929-1971. Metuchen, N.J.: Scarecrow Press, 1973. 245p.
(Author Bibliography Series, No. 1).

   Professor Hayashi provides a revised and expanded
edition of his 1967 bibliography, which has become a
standard source for the period covered. This edition
continues the English language orientation and absence
of annotations but simplifies and improves the arrangement of citations. Hayashi attempts to list all known
primary and secondary sources published in the English
language up to mid-1972. Part I lists 379 items by
Steinbeck; Part II lists the secondary materials (1,800
items broken down by type of work). There is a very
useful index to authors of the secondary materials and
the Steinbeck titles to which they refer.

1. Adaptations. 2. Bibliography. 3. Book Reviews.
4. Correspondence. 5. Criticism and Interpretation.
6. Dissertations, Academic. 7. Film Reviews. 8. Manuscripts. 9. Plays. 10. Poetry. 11. Short Stories.
12. Speeches.

88. Hayashi, Tetsumaro. A New Steinbeck Bibliography:
1971-1981. Metuchen, N.J.: Scarecrow Press, 1983. 147p.
(Scarecrow Author Bibliographies, No. 64).

   Basically this work is a revised and updated version
of his earlier A New Steinbeck Bibliography: 1929-1971
(see: No. 87). There are 1,080 entries representing
materials published or reprinted in English of a scholarly
and critical nature. Organization remains the same as
his previous work--primary and secondary sources.
There are further subdivisions in each general section,
covering such areas as novels, short stories, plays,
letters, etc. There is an introduction by Steinbeck ex-
pert Robert DeMott that focuses Hayashi's work in terms
of suggesting future directions for Steinbeck criticism.
Concluding the volume are two appendixes and a chronology of Steinbeck's life and works.

1. Adaptations. 2. Bibliographies. 3. Bibliography.
4. Book Reviews. 5. Correspondence. 6. Criticism and

Interpretation.   7. Dissertations, Academic.   8. Film
Reviews.   9. Manuscripts.   10. Plays.   11. Poetry.
12. Short Stories.   13. Speeches.

89.   Hayashi, Tetsumaro.   "A Selected Checklist of Recent
Books on Steinbeck Published in the United States."   Steinbeck Quarterly, 13 (Winter-Spring 1980), 61-62.
        This brief checklist includes five primary sources or
    newly published Steinbeck titles.   Also there are some
    studies of a critical nature included in this list.

    1. Bibliography.   2. Criticism and Interpretation.

90.   Hayashi, Tetsumaro.   The Special Steinbeck Collection
of the Ball State University Library: A Bibliographical
Handbook [With Donald L. Siefker] Muncie, Ind.:   The John
Steinbeck Society of America, English Dept., Ball State
University, 1972.   30p.
        This work attempts to list and briefly describe the
    Steinbeck materials held in the Special Collections De-
    partment, the General Collections, and the Professional
    Collection of the Ball State University Library.   The
    basic organization is by primary and secondary sources
    within these collections.   Also included are see refer-
    ences to facilitate use.   In all, there are 446 items cited
    within this work, covering most types of materials pub-
    lished by and about Steinbeck.

    1. Archives.   2. Bibliography.   3. Ball State University
    Library--Catalogs.   4. Library Resources.

91.   Hayashi, Tetsumaro, ed. and comp.   Steinbeck and
Hemingway: Dissertation Abstracts and Research Opportuni-
ties.   Metuchen, N.J.:   Scarecrow Press, 1980.   228p.
        Essentially this compilation reprints all of the ab-
    stracts written for the dissertations on Steinbeck and
    Hemingway that were printed in Dissertation Abstracts/
    Dissertation Abstracts International (see: No. 47) up to
    1977.   The 40 abstracts of Steinbeck dissertations are
    covered in the first part of the volume.   On pages 67-77
    Richard F. Peterson provides an essay entitled: "The
    Keepers of the Flame: Past Research and Research Op-

portunities in Steinbeck Graduate Studies." The volume
concludes with a variety of indexes including dissertation
authors and directors, subject, title, university, and
chronological.

1. Dissertations, Academic--Abstracts. 2. History and
Criticism.

92. Hayashi, Tetsumaro, ed. Steinbeck's Literary Dimension:
A Guide to Comparative Studies. Metuchen, N.J.: Scarecrow
Press, 1973. 191p.
     This compilation is a collection of eleven essays by
various authorities comparing Steinbeck with other prominent writers such as Dickens, Faulkner, Hemingway,
and others. These essays are accompanied by reviews
of scholarship by Peter Lisca and the editor. Professor
Lisca, on pages 148-167, presents an extensive bibliographical essay covering Steinbeck criticism up to
1971. On pages 168-173, Dr. Hayashi details recent
trends in Steinbeck scholarship in the United States.
In this survey he lists book-length studies arranged
chronologically and some works in preparation at that
time. On pages 174-179, Dr. Hayashi provides a selected
bibliography. Part I lists doctoral dissertations (1946-
1969), arranged chronologically. Part II lists critical
articles since 1945, arranged alphabetically by author.

1. Criticism and Interpretation. 2. Dissertations, Academic.

93. Hayashi, Tetsumaro, ed. A Study Guide To Steinbeck:
A Handbook to His Major Works (Part I and Part II).
Metuchen, N.J.: Scarecrow Press, 1974; 1979. 2v.
     Designed as a study guide for classroom teachers,
librarians, and students, this work (currently in two
volumes), is geared to offer advice, suggestions,
methods, and sources so that users can explore on their
own the untouched regions of Steinbeck's writing. Each
discussion, written by a specialist, begins with a back-
ground of the work and provides a critique and plot
synopsis, suggestions for classroom discussions, sug-
gested topics for term papers, and a selected bibliography, many of them annotated. This is an extremely
useful compilation.

1. America and Americans--Criticism and Interpretation.
2. Bibliography. 3. Burning Bright--Criticism and
Interpretation. 4. Cannery Row--Criticism and Interpretation. 5. Criticism and Interpretation. 6. Cup of
Gold--Criticism and Interpretation. 7. East of Eden--
Criticism and Interpretation. 8. Film Adaptations.
9. The Grapes of Wrath--Criticism and Interpretation.
10. In Dubious Battle--Criticism and Interpretation. 11.
The Log from the Sea of Cortez--Criticism and Interpretation. 12. The Long Valley--Criticism and Interpretation. 13. The Moon Is Down--Criticism and Interpretation. 14. Moving-Picture Plays. 15. Of Mice and Men--
Criticism and Interpretation. 16. Of Mice and Men
(Play)--Criticism and Interpretation. 17. The Pastures
of Heaven--Criticism and Interpretation. 18. The Pearl--
Criticism and Interpretation. 19. A Russian Journal--
Criticism and Interpretation. 20. Sea of Cortez--Criti-
cism and Interpretation. 21. Study and Teaching--
Outlines, Syllabi, etc. 22. Sweet Thursday--Criticism
and Interpretation. 23. To a God Unknown--Criticism
and Interpretation. 24. Tortilla Flat--Criticism and
Interpretation. 25. Travels with Charley--Criticism
and Interpretation. 26. Viva Zapata! (Moving picture)--Criticism and Interpretation. 27. The Wayward
Bus--Criticism and Interpretation. 28. The Winter of
Our Discontent--Criticism and Interpretation.

94. Hidekazu, Hirose. "Japanese Steinbeck Criticism in
1971." Steinbeck Quarterly, 6 (Fall 1973), 99-104.
     The author covers nine critical articles on Steinbeck
that were published in Japanese sources during 1971.

     1. Criticism and Interpretation--Japan.

95. Hidekazu, Hirose. "Japanese Steinbeck Criticism in
1972-73." Steinbeck Quarterly, 8 (Spring 1975), 56-59.
     This bibliographical essay discusses eighteen articles
on Steinbeck published in Japan during 1972-1973. The
reviewer apparently feels that the articles reviewed
make little contribution to Steinbeck studies in general.

     1. Criticism and Interpretation--Japan.

96. Hidekazu, Hirose. "Japanese Steinbeck Criticism in
1974-1975." Steinbeck Quarterly, 10 (Spring 1977), 44-48.
    This critical survey discusses some thirty articles
    about Steinbeck appearing in Japanese scholarly journals
    during 1974-1975.

    1. Criticism and Interpretation--Japan.

97. Hilton, William C. "John Steinbeck: An Annotated Bibliography of Criticism, 1936-1963." An MA Thesis. Detroit:
Wayne State University, 1965. 88 leaves.
    This unpublished master's thesis is actually in the
    form of a bibliographical essay except for two checklists
    on leaves 69-87. Source abbreviations used throughout
    the text are listed on leaves ii-iv. Following the intro-
    duction there are chapters covering bibliographies,
    biography, ideas, criticism in general, and one covering
    criticism of specific works such as: The Long Valley,
    In Dubious Battle, Of Mice and Men, The Grapes of
    Wrath, The Moon Is Down, Cannery Row, The Wayward
    Bus, The Pearl, Burning Bright, East of Eden, and
    Sweet Thursday. The first checklist is arranged alpha-
    betically by author and provides the bibliographic infor-
    mation on full length critical studies. The second check-
    list is organized in the same way and contains the same
    kind of information for essays. There is a brief index
    listing the major Steinbeck titles covered in the bibliog-
    raphy in alphabetical order on leaf 88.

    1. Bibliographies. 2. Biography. 3. Criticism and
    Interpretation.

98. Howard, Patsy C., comp. and ed. Theses in American
Literature, 1896-1971. Ann Arbor, MI: Pierian Press, 1973.
307p.
    Master's theses are a valuable source of information
    for students of literature. This work includes references
    to over 7,000 unpublished baccalaureate and master's
    theses from more than two hundred universities and col-
    leges, mainly in the United States and Canada. It is
    arranged alphabetically by author. Under each entry
    the theses are alphabetized by the author of the thesis.
    The entries include basic bibliographic information indi-

cating the title of the thesis or essay, degree, name
of granting institution, date, and at times, the number
of pages in the thesis. Access is provided by author
and "limited subject" indexes. Since this listing is
not exhaustive and the period scanned ends in 1971
the user should consult other sources for more current
coverage. Also you should be aware that some of the
granting institutions have changed name, for example
some colleges are now universities. Theses related to
John Steinbeck are found mainly on pages 203-206,
items 5469-5561. See also items 40 (p.2); 1551 (p.59);
1582 (p.71); and 6540 (p.241) for Steinbeck related
theses.

1. Theses, Academic.

99. Humanities Index. New York: H. W. Wilson, 1974-
V. 1- . (Formerly: The Social Sciences and Humanities
Index (April 1965-March 1974, Vols. 19-27; Formerly: International Index to Periodicals (1907-March 1965, Vols. 1-18).
      This major index to scholarly journals is arranged
in two parts: (1) an author/subject index to periodicals publishing articles in the humanities, and (2) a
list of book reviews published in those periodicals and
arranged alphabetically under the names of the authors
of the books reviewed. Includes literary authors'
names as subjects and other subject categories. Starting with Volume 8, for scholarly articles about Steinbeck, simply look under his name.

1. Criticism and Interpretation--Periodicals--Indexes.

100. An Index to Book Reviews in the Humanities. Wil-
liamson, MI: Phillip Thomson, 1960- . V. 1- .
      For the purpose of this work, the humanities include
biography, personal narratives, memoirs, philosophy,
and history up to 1970, when coverage was dropped.
Approximately three hundred periodicals and newspapers
are scanned for this author only index. To locate
Steinbeck related book reviews, simply look under his
name.

1. Book Reviews--Indexes.

101. Index to Little Magazines. Chicago: Swallow Press,
1949- . (Publisher varies: Started with Alan Swallow in
Denver. Frequency also varies.)
     This work is a comprehensive index to articles and
     reviews published in American little magazines. It is
     arranged as a single-alphabet author/title list. For
     interpretative articles on Steinbeck simply look under
     his name in each volume. See also: Comprehensive
     Index to English-Language Little Magazines, (31) edited
     by Marion Sader.

     1. Criticism and Interpretation--Periodicals--Indexes.

102. Index Translationum ... International Bibliography of
Translations. Paris: UNESCO (United Nations Educational,
Scientific and Cultural Organization), 1949- . V. 1- .
     Two series comprise this set. The first covers the
     period 1932-1940, Vols. 1-31, and was published quar-
     terly. The new series (1949-to date) is published an-
     nually, however, as with most United Nations publica-
     tions, it is several years behind in coverage. For
     example Vol. 31 covering 1978 was published in 1982.
     It offers multiple access to translations published
     throughout the world. Translations are listed by
     country of publication as well as under ten major subject
     headings. Separate indexes by author, publisher, and
     translator are also provided. Entries include full bib-
     liographic information, including original language, title,
     publisher, and date. To locate Steinbeck titles scan the
     "Alphabetical List of Principal Authors" under his name.
     You will probably find some abbreviations for Steinbeck
     titles for the country and the item number (e.g., BRA
     44, meaning Brazil, Item No. 44). Then find this
     country in the body of the bibliography and under
     "Literature" locate the item number for this particular
     translation. This process may seem a little tedious but
     it is well worth it if you need a particular Steinbeck
     title in a foreign language.

     1. Translations.

103. International Steinbeck Congress, 1st, Kyushu University, 1976. John Steinbeck, East and West: Proceedings of

the First International Steinbeck Congress Held at Kyushu
University, Fukuoka City, Japan, in August 1976. Edited
by Tetsumaro Hayashi, Yasuo Hashiguchi, and Richard F.
Peterson. Muncie, IN: Steinbeck Society of America,
English Dept., Ball State University, 1978. 95p. (Steinbeck
Monograph Series, No. 8).

    The proceedings of this conference indicate the
broad scope of Steinbeck related research that is being
conducted in both east and west scholarly environments.
Even though there is no formal bibliography, each of
the essays contains a wealth of bibliographic information that will be of value to Steinbeck researchers.

1. Congresses.   2. Criticism and Interpretation.

104.   Jain, Sunita. John Steinbeck's Concept of Man: A
Critical Study of His Novels. New Delhi, India: New States-
man Publishing Co., [1979]. 102p.

    This work by an Indian scholar analyzes Steinbeck's
novels and argues that they "show a mind and art, not
satisfied with fragments or corrupted by fame or riches,
relentlessly seeking to understand and depict life in its
varied forms until Steinbeck was able to etch unreason-
ably his image of man." (Dust Jacket) The selected
bibliography on pages 99-101 is divided into the tradi-
tional primary and secondary sources. The first section is arranged alphabetically by title and the second
alphabetically by author.

1. Bibliography.   2. Criticism and Interpretation.

105.   The John Steinbeck Society of Japan Newsletter.
Okayoma City, Japan: The Society, 1978- . No. 1- .

    The first issue of this newsletter was published in
May of 1978 and has been issued annually in this month
since then. Each issue usually includes short pieces of
Japanese and American Steinbeck specialists. Many of
these are in English. Reports of meetings, special
events, and Steinbeck related publications are often
included as regular features. This newsletter is a
valuable source for notices of Japanese translations of
Steinbeck's works and related criticism.

1. Bibliography.   2. Periodicals.

106. Johnson, Merle DeVore. <u>Merle Johnson's American</u>
<u>First Editions</u>. 4th edition. Revised and enlarged by Jacob
Blanck. New York: Bowker, 1942. Also reprinted:
Waltham, MA: Mark Press, 1969. 523p.

> For many years this work has been the standard
> source for identifying first editions by booksellers. It
> is arranged alphabetically by author. Under each name
> the titles of their major works are listed in chronological
> sequence. For each entry title, place of publication,
> and date of publication are provided. Additional bib-
> liographical information is given for some titles. There
> is some biographical information for most authors at the
> end of each section. Pages 472-473 list thirteen
> Steinbeck first editions up to 1941 and a few other re-
> lated titles. For each of the first editions some publica-
> tion information is given.

> 1. Book Collecting. 2. First Editions.

107. Jones, Lawrence William. <u>John Steinbeck as Fabulist</u>.
Muncie, IN: John Steinbeck Society of America, English
Dept., Ball State University, 1973. 35p. (Steinbeck Mon-
ograph Series, No. 3).

> Jones explores the latter half of Steinbeck's career
> and analyzes the fabulistic qualities in his writing.
> There is no bibliography per se in this monograph, how-
> ever, the bibliographical notes are excellent sources of
> information in this area of Steinbeck studies.

> 1. Criticism and Interpretation.

108. Kalich, Roseann. "An Index and Annotated Bibliography of Nonbook Materials in the Steinbeck Collection of the
John Steinbeck Library in Salinas, California." An MA Research Paper. San Jose, CA: Dept. of Librarianship, San
Jose State University, July 1975. 105 leaves.

> The main purpose of this unpublished research paper
> in the form of an index is to provide access to this im-
> portant collection for students and scholars doing re-
> search on John Steinbeck. The nonbook materials un-
> der consideration consist of newspaper clippings, mag-
> azine articles, articles from reference books, photo-
> graphs, and miscellaneous materials. The body of this

work is organized into eight chapters. Chapter One,
outlines the scope of the study and its purpose.
Chapter Two, discusses Steinbeck and his career in
general. Chapter Three contains sixty annotations
from articles appearing in the Salinas Index Journal,
and the Salinas Californian, both local newspapers.
Chapter Four has thirty-nine citations from articles
in other California newspapers such as: Carmel Pine
Cone, Monterey Peninsula Herald, Register-Pajaronian
(Watsonville), San Jose Mercury News, San Francisco
Chronicle, San Francisco Examiner, Oakland Tribune,
and the Los Angeles Times. A few original sources
could not be identified but appear to have been from
a California newspaper. Chapter Five includes thirty
citations from magazine articles. These are listed
chronologically and then alphabetically by title if
there is more than one article from an issue. Chapter
Six lists eighteen citations of articles from newspapers
outside of California, magazine articles having no
source, articles from biographical dictionaries, and
articles in collected works. Materials not from periodical sources are arranged alphabetically by book title
following the periodical annotation. Chapter Seven has
thirteen entries covering miscellaneous biographical
materials. This includes Steinbeck's Commencement
Program from Salinas High School, articles from the
high school yearbook El Gabilan, statements and cer-
tificate regarding Steinbeck's birth, plus photographs
not included in periodicals. Chapter Eight discusses
the growing interest of the city of Salinas in John
Steinbeck. A bibliography of sources is included on
leaves 80-81. The Appendix contains sample bibliography working cards and samples of interview questions used in compiling this research paper. There
are two indexes. The first is a cross reference index
to the Steinbeck collection that lists the number of citations in numerical sequence, the title of the article
or item, volume, and page number in which it can be
found in the biography category of the Steinbeck collection. The second index is an alphabetical listing by
name and title.

1. Bibliography. 2. Carmel Pine Cone (Newspaper)--
Indexes. 3. Los Angeles Times (Newspaper)--Indexes.
4. Monterey Peninsula Herald (Newspaper)--Indexes.

5. Oakland Tribune (Newspaper)--Indexes. 6. Reg-
ister-Pajaronian [Watsonville] (Newspaper)--Indexes.
7. Salinas Californian (Newspaper)--Indexes. 8.
Salinas Index-Journal (Newspaper)--Indexes. 9. San
Francisco Chronicle (Newspaper)--Indexes. 10. San
Francisco Examiner (Newspaper)--Indexes. 11. San
Jose Mercury News (Newspaper)--Indexes. 12. Salinas
Public Library--Nonbook Materials--Indexes. 13. El
Gabilan (Yearbook).

109. Kennedy, Barbara Maxine. "John Ernst Steinbeck:
An Annotated Bibliography of His Personal Correspondence
in the Manuscript Collections of the Bancroft Library." An
MA Research Paper. San Jose, CA: Dept. of Librarianship,
California State University, San Jose, June 1974. 58 leaves.
    The Bancroft Library at the University of California,
Berkeley, is the repository of many fine collections relating to Western America, including collections of
authors like John Steinbeck. There are many first and
special editions of his works, some manuscripts, a collection of photographs, and close to 300 original letters
which provide unique material for use by students and
scholars. This unpublished research paper was prepared to assist researchers in the use of this material
by providing access via a systematic listing. The letters listed cover most of Steinbeck's writing career,
roughly from 1929 to 1963. Entries in this bibliography
are arranged chronologically. Unfortunately Steinbeck
often did not date his letters; consequently, it has been
necessary to supply approximate dates to many letters
on the basis of content. These questionable dates have
been bracketed to distinguish them from those letters
actually dated by Steinbeck. The index on leaves 52-
58 will assist the user by providing access to this collection by subject, chiefly place names, individuals,
and titles of Steinbeck's works. Unfortunately, it was
extremely difficult to ascertain full names for casual
references in the letters, so the user is advised to consult the alphabetical listings under both first and last
names. Spelling problems may also be encountered due
to the difficulty of interpreting Steinbeck's handwriting.
The format for the entries include descriptive information from each letter, the recipient's name, mailing location, date, number of leaves comprising the letter,

and a note relative to whether it is a holograph or
typescript document. The manuscript classification
numbers and relatively small number of correspondents
are provided on leaf 6.

1. Bancroft Library, University of California, Berkeley
--Manuscripts.   2. Correspondence.

109a. Kiernan, Thomas. The Intricate Music: A Biography
of John Steinbeck. Boston: Little, Brown, 1979. 331p.
        Receiving some severe criticism from a number of
reviewers, this biography attempts to reveal Steinbeck's life as it relates to his development as a writer.
On pages 318-319 there is a classified checklist of the
works of John Steinbeck arranged under the categories
of fiction, nonfiction, plays, a documentary, and a
screenplay. The notes on pages 320-324 carry additional references to other biographical material.

1. Bibliography.   2. Biography.

110.   Kolar, Carol Koehmstedt. Plot Summary Index.   2nd
ed., revised and enlarged. Metuchen, N.J.: Scarecrow
Press, 1981. 526p.
        Indexed here are 110 collections of plot summaries
covering over 225 volumes. Access is by title of the
work and/or by author. Entries provide citations to
the collection or collections in which a summary has
been published. In the author section on page 495
there is a list of eleven Steinbeck titles. Each of
these titles was listed previously, in alphabetical order, in the title section on pages 2, 35, 78, 108, 131,
185, 198, 234, 272, 285, and 306 respectively. There
is an abbreviation following each title that indicates
the source or sources of a plot summary and the page
on which it appears. One must consult the key to abbreviations in the front of the volume for titles of the
sources indexed.

1. Bibliography.   2. Plots--Indexes.

111.   Kolb, Harold H. A Field Guide to the Study of American

<u>Literature</u>. Charlottesville: University Press of Virginia,
1976. 136p.

Intended as an annotated guide to American literature. The "Author, subject, and genre index" includes
names of individual authors mentioned in the annotations. This guide lists a number of works that either
contain information about Steinbeck or bibliographies of
his works. These works include item 12 on page 5,
items 47 and 48 on pages 17-18, item 272 on pages 98-
99, item 278 on page 100, and item 344 on page 116.

1. Bibliographies. 2. Criticism and Interpretation.

112. Koster, Donald Nelson. <u>American Literature and</u>
<u>Language: A Guide to Information Sources</u>. Detroit: Gale
Research Co., 1982. 396p. (American studies information
guide series, Vol. 13; Gale information guide library).

As a selected guide to secondary sources of information about American literature and language, this
work annotates 1,885 books in English. The bibliography has two main sections plus author, title, and
subject indexes. Part 1, devoted to literature, contains citations on general aids, separately grouping in
sequence, by author, bibliographies, checklists, indexes, and reference guides; biographical reference
aids; general histories; literary histories; and general
critical studies. These are followed by alphabetically
arranged individual author bibliographies. Part 2 lists
thirty titles relating to dictionaries, usage, dialects,
and pronunciation. In most cases, annotations are
descriptive, evaluative, and brief. Biographical, bibliographical, and critical works about Steinbeck are
found on pages 246-250, Items: 1495-1520. Check this
subject index for several other works that mention
Steinbeck.

1. Bibliographies. 2. Biography. 3. Criticism and
Interpretation.

113. Kunitz, Stanley J., ed. <u>Twentieth Century Authors:</u>
<u>A Biographical Dictionary of Modern Literature</u> [Edited with
Howard Haycraft]. New York: H. W. Wilson Co., 1942.
1,577p.

This standard biographical work carries a sketch of
Steinbeck's career on pages 1338-1339. At the conclusion of this sketch is a brief bibliography listing principal works by and about Steinbeck.

1. Bibliography. 2. Biography. 3. Criticism and Interpretation.

114. Kunitz, Stanley J., ed. Twentieth Century Authors:
A Biographical Dictionary of Modern Literature. First Supplement. [Edited with Vineta Colby] New York: H. W.
Wilson Co., 1955. 1123p.
      More biographical material is included on pages
954-955 about Steinbeck. There is another brief bibliography covering additional works by and critical
materials about Steinbeck on page 955.

1. Bibliography. 2. Biography. 3. Criticism and
Interpretation.

115. LaPlante, Kathleen Rosanne. "A Descriptive Bibliog-
raphy of Three of the John Steinbeck Novels Included in the
Steinbeck Collection of the Library of the California State
University at San Jose." An MA Research Paper. San Jose,
CA: Dept. of Librarianship, California State University, San
Jose, July 1972. 58 leaves.
      This unpublished research paper is a descriptive
bibliography covering The Pastures of Heaven (1932),
Tortilla Flat (1935), and The Grapes of Wrath (1939)
in twelve different editions or impressions. Extensive
descriptions are provided for each edition. A bibliog-
raphy of source materials is given on leaf 58.

1. The Pastures of Heaven. 2. Tortilla Flat. 3. The
Grapes of Wrath.

116. Leary, Lewis Gaston. Articles on American Literature,
1900-1950. Durham, N.C.: Duke University Press, 1954.
437p.
      This compilation is a bibliography of articles and
significant reviews on American literature. Arrangement is classified, with categories such as "Almanacs,

Annuals, and Giftbooks," "Prose," etc. Within each
section the arrangement is alphabetical by subject, including authors as subjects. A list of critical articles
about Steinbeck is found on pages 278-279. They are
arranged alphabetically by author.

1. Criticism and Interpretation.

117.   Leary, Lewis Gaston.   Articles on American Literature,
1950-1967.   [With Carolyn Bartholet and Catharine Roth]
Durham, N.C.:   Duke University Press, 1970.   751p.
Consists of a bibliography of articles and significant
reviews continuing the author's earlier work for the
period, 1900-1950. A list of critical articles about
Steinbeck is found on pages 492-496. They are arranged alphabetically by author.

1. Criticism and Interpretation.

118.   Leary, Lewis Gaston.   Articles on American Literature,
1968-1975.   [With John Auchard] Durham, N.C.:   Duke University Press, 1979.   745p.
Consists of a bibliography of articles and significant
reviews continuing the author's work for the period
1950-1967. A list of critical articles about Steinbeck is
found on pages 466-471. They are arranged alphabetically by author.

1. Criticism and Interpretation.

119.   Levant, Howard.   The Novels of John Steinbeck: A
Critical Study.   With an introduction by Warren G. French.
Columbia: University of Missouri Press, 1974.   304p.
This work is a study of Steinbeck's fiction in terms
of his use of "dramatic" and "panoramic" techniques,
especially as these relate to his increasing problems in
finding adequate forms in which to embody fictionally
his philosophy. The bibliography, located on pages
303-304, includes selected works by John Steinbeck.
This checklist type bibliography lists books, along with
articles and essays in chronological sequence.

1. Bibliography.

120. Libman, Valentia A. Russian Studies of American
Literature: A Bibliography. Translated by Robert V. Allen,
edited by Clarence Gohdes. Chapel Hill, N.C.: University
of North Carolina Press, 1969. 218p.
>   The entries in this bibliography are given in trans-
>   literation, with titles of books and periodical articles
>   in both transliteration and English translation. A gen-
>   eral section, chronologically arranged, is followed by
>   sections for individual authors. An index of American
>   authors is provided, but none listing critics. The
>   bibliography on pages 176-179 is a chronological check-
>   list of materials by and about Steinbeck including Rus-
>   sian translations of his major works.
>
>   1. Criticism and Interpretation--Russia. 2. Transla-
>   tions, Russian.

121. Liedloff, Helmut. Steinbeck in German Translation: A
Study of Translational Practices. Carbondale, IL: Southern
Illinois University Press, 1965. 104p. (Monographs in the
Sciences, Social Studies, and Humanities: Humanities Series,
No. 1).
>   This study is a comparison of the texts of Stein-
>   beck's The Grapes of Wrath (1939), Cannery Row
>   (1945), The Red Pony (1937), and the short story
>   "The Chrysanthemums," with their translations into
>   German which is calculated to evaluate and call atten-
>   tion to the general problems involved. Appendix B
>   on pages 96-100 is an alphabetical list by title of Ger-
>   man translations of Steinbeck's works published between
>   1940 and 1961. Under each title is listed one or more
>   translations. The bibliography on pages 101-104 lists
>   a number of books and articles by and about Steinbeck.
>   This list is arranged in alphabetical order by author.
>
>   1. Bibliography. 2. Criticism and Interpretation--Ger-
>   many. 3. Translations, German.

122. Lisca, Peter. "Bibliography." IN: Steinbeck, John.
The Grapes of Wrath, Text and Criticism, edited by Peter
Lisca. New York: Viking Press, 1972. Reissued in paper-
back by Penguin Books, New York, 1977. 881p. (The
Viking Critical Library).

This resetting of the text of the novel is accompanied by some hitherto unpublished Steinbeck letters and a variety of criticism of the novel. The bibliography associated with this edition is found on pages 869-881. The first section covers works by Steinbeck including fiction, nonfiction, plays, film stories, and scripts. These lists are arranged chronologically. The next major section covers criticism. The first part deals with general materials about Steinbeck including books and periodicals. This is followed by a section on The Grapes of Wrath itself including books and periodical articles. These sections are all arranged alphabetically by author.

1. Bibliography. 2. Correspondence. 3. Criticism and Interpretation. 4. Film Adaptations. 5. The Grapes of Wrath--Criticism and Interpretation. 6. Plays.

123. Lisca, Peter. John Steinbeck, Nature and Myth. New York: Crowell, 1978. 245p.
This work is aimed primarily at the new, younger generation of Steinbeck readers. It is intended to be a thorough and informative introduction to Steinbeck's writing and the many themes and techniques he developed during his career. The selected bibliography is located on pages 237-239. The first section lists works by Steinbeck including his fictional, nonfictional, and posthumous works. Materials in each of these sections are arranged chronologically. The second section lists books about Steinbeck in alphabetical order by author.

1. Bibliography. 2. Criticism and Interpretation.

124. Lisca, Peter. The Wide World of John Steinbeck. New edition. New York: Gordian Press, 1981. 334p.
First published in 1958 this work is still considered one of the most thorough and detailed studies of Steinbeck's fiction. This new edition adds an "afterword" by Professor Lisca giving it more currency. There is "A Working Checklist of Steinbeck's Published Work" on pages 318-322. This checklist includes books by Steinbeck, critical studies appearing in periodicals and

newspapers, and a list of miscellaneous items.

1. Bibliography.   2. Criticism and Interpretation.

125.   Literary Writings in America: A Bibliography. Mill-
wood, N.Y.: KTO Press, 1977. 8v.
         This multivolume work is a photoreproduction of a
card file prepared at the University of Pennsylvania
under the auspices of the Works Progress Administra-
tion, 1938-42. Entries are arranged alphabetically by
literary author, with sections for separate works,
periodical publications, biography, and criticism as
applicable. Signed book reviews are entered under the
name of the reviewer as well as under the name of the
author of the book. In Volume 7, pages 9421-9422,
there is a list of books and articles by and about
Steinbeck including some reviews.

1. Bibliography.   2. Criticism and Interpretation.

126.   McCarthy, Paul. John Steinbeck. New York:
Frederick Ungar Publishing Co., 1980. 163p.
         This work is a general study of Steinbeck and his
fictional works. The bibliography on pages 153-158 is
divided into two main sections. The first is a list of
works by Steinbeck arranged in alphabetical sequence
by title. The list of 38 titles includes books, articles,
and some short stories. The second section is a list
of 49 critical books and articles about Steinbeck arranged alphabetically by author.

1. Bibliography.   2. Criticism and Interpretation.

127.   Macleod, Gwen. "The complete criticisms of John
Steinbeck's The Grapes of Wrath, 1939-1972: An Annotated
Bibliography." An MA Research Paper. San Jose, CA:
Dept. of Librarianship, California State University, San Jose,
January 1973. 81 leaves.
         The purpose of this unpublished research paper is
to present an extensive list of criticism published on
The Grapes of Wrath up to 1972 appearing in all types
of sources. In the main section of this bibliography

the entries are arranged in strict alphabetical order by
author or title. Unsigned and nontitled articles are
listed by the title of the source in which they appear.
Annotations are provided for many of the citations. An
introductory chapter entitled "Data Analysis" traces the
impact of various types of criticism on the reception of
The Grapes of Wrath. There is a bibliography of
sources used on leaves 78-81.

1. The Grapes of Wrath--Criticism and Interpretation.

128. Magazine Index. Belmont, CA: Information Access
Corporation, 1977- .
     Like the Readers' Guide to Periodical Literature
(156) this service scans the popular literature in over
400 periodicals to make up this index. The main difference is that it is in a microfilm format contained
within a microfilm reader that scans back and forth
very rapidly to the subject desired. A new film is
issued monthly and contains a 5 year cumulation. The
years prior to the cumulation are available on microfiche
back to 1977. Online Version: The online version of
this index (File 47) is available on the DIALOG system
and goes back to 1959. The extensive indexing makes
this a valuable service. Since both versions treat
authors as subjects, you simply look under Steinbeck
to find popular articles about him.

1. Criticism and Interpretation--Periodicals--Indexes.

129. Magill, Frank Northern. Magill's Bibliography of Literary Criticism: Selected Sources for the Study of More
Than 2,500 Outstanding Works on Western Literature. As-
sociate Editors Stephen L. Hanson and Patricia King Hanson.
Englewood Cliffs, N.J.: Salem Press, 1979. 4v.
     This work is an extensive listing of critical material
on many authors, both past and present. The critical
articles and books on Steinbeck are found in Volume 4
on pages 1993-2005. This bibliography is arranged under title of the work starting with Cannery Row (1945)
and alphabetically through The Winter of Our Discontent
(1961). The critical works are listed alphabetically by
author under each title.

1. Criticism and Interpretation.

130. Marks, Lester Jay. Thematic Design in the Novels of
John Steinbeck. The Hague: Mouton, 1969. 144p. (Studies
in American Literature, v. 11).
        In this study, the author makes a valuable contribu-
    tion to the understanding of John Steinbeck's fictive
    design. There is a bibliography located on pages 138-
    142. It consists of two major sections. The first
    covers works by Steinbeck under the categories of
    books and selected articles, essays, and letters. En-
    tries in each of these divisions are arranged in chron-
    ological order. The second major section lists selected
    criticism with entries arranged alphabetically by author
    or title.

    1. Bibliography.   2. Criticism and Interpretation.

131. Marr, Celestine. "John Steinbeck's The Pastures of
Heaven, The Red Pony, and In Dubious Battle: An Annotated
Bibliography of Critical Writings on Three Early Works." An
MA Research Paper. San Jose, CA: Dept. of Librarianship,
San Jose State University, December 1975. 81 leaves.
        This unpublished research paper was prepared as a
    useful tool in the study of Steinbeck's early novels. It
    is extensive, but not exhaustive because many fugitive
    materials are not discovered by the compiler. The body
    of this bibliography consists of six major units. Chap-
    ters One and Two contain introductory material.
    Chapters Three through Five provide the bibliographies
    of each of the books under consideration within which
    the criticism is divided into three separate categories:
    criticism in books, criticism in periodicals, and book re-
    views. Chapter Six contains a checklist of master's
    theses and doctoral dissertations. Except for Chapter
    Six all of the entries in the bibliographies are well an-
    notated. The sources used to select items for these
    bibliographies are discussed in the introduction.

    1. Dissertations, Academic.   2. The Pastures of Heaven
    --Criticism and Interpretation.   3. The Red Pony--Crit-
    icism and Interpretation.   4. In Dubious Battle--Criti-
    cism and Interpretation.   5. Theses, Academic.

132. <u>Masters Abstracts</u>. Ann Arbor, MI: University Microfilms International, 1962- . V. 1- .
      Only a small number of American colleges and uni-
versities cooperate in this quarterly reference service
for master's theses. Entries are arranged by subject
discipline such as Literature, American. Within each
subject category, entries are arranged alphabetically by
author. Each issue has an author index, with a Cumulative Subject Index and a Cumulative Author Index in
the final issue of each volume. Because of the limited
participation in this project, not many theses on or relating to John Steinbeck are to be found in this work.
(See also: 133).

1. Theses, Academic--Abstracts.

133. <u>Master's Theses in the Arts and Social Sciences</u>.   Cedar
Falls, IA: Research Publications, 1977. V. 1- .
      Theses reported in this annual publication exclude
the areas of Education and the Pure and Applied
Sciences. Those listed are arranged into nearly three
dozen subject categories which are listed in the Table
of Contents. Access is provided via the author and
institutional indexes. The Institutional Index assigns a
code number to each institution as well as showing the
serial number of each thesis accepted by the institution.
Each entry for a thesis gives the serial number assigned
to it, the name of the author, the title of the thesis,
and in parentheses following the end of the title, the
code number of the institution that accepted it. If you
are looking for theses about John Steinbeck, you must
scan the subject category of English and Literature from
beginning to end. Unfortunately there is no easier way
to locate relevant theses. The coverage, however, is
much better than <u>Masters Abstracts</u>, (See: 132).

1. Theses, Academic.

134. Millett, Fred Benjamin.   <u>Contemporary American Authors:
A Critical Survey and 219 Bio-Bibliographies</u>.   New York:
Harcourt, Brace and Co., 1940. 716p.
      Arranged to provide (1) a critical survey of contem-
porary literature, (2) 219 short biographies with brief

primary and secondary bibliographies, and (3) selected
readings. John Steinbeck is treated on pages 596-597.
Following a brief biographical sketch there is a short
checklist of novels, short stories, the play Of Mice and
Men, and the social study "Their Blood Is Strong."
This section is followed by a listing of studies and
articles about Steinbeck including several bibliographies.

1. Bibliographies. 2. Bibliography. 3. Biography.
4. Criticism and Interpretation. 5. Of Mice and Men
(Play). 6. Their Blood Is Strong.

135. Millichap, Joseph R. Steinbeck and Film. New York:
Frederick Ungar Publishing Co., 1983. 205p.
        From the beginning, film was to have a marked in-
fluence on Steinbeck's work both for good and bad.
His major novels were written under the impact of the
documentary realism that sprang from the nation's Depression mood, and his decline can be traced to the
social changes brought on by World War II, and to the
fact that Steinbeck began to write with at least one eye
on a likely screen adaptation. (Dust Jacket) There
is a "Selected Bibliography" on pages 191-194. Section
I, lists works by John Steinbeck, further subdivided
in the categories of fiction, nonfiction, plays, film
stories and screenplays. Section II, is a list of secondary sources of general and specific critical works.
On pages 195-199 is a "Filmography" of thirteen Steinbeck film adaptations.

1. Bibliography. 2. Film Adaptations. 3. Moving-
Picture Plays. 4. Moving-Picture Plays and Literature.

136. Mitchell Books. John Steinbeck [Catalog Six]. Pasa-
dena, CA: Mitchell Books, 1982. 68p.
        Originally issued as a booksellers' catalog this work
contains much bibliographic detail of value to Steinbeck
specialists as well as book collectors. Listed are 204
items covering the following types of materials: Books
and Pamphlets By John Steinbeck, listed alphabetically
by title; Books with Contributions By John Steinbeck,
listed chronologically; Contributions to Periodicals By
John Steinbeck, also arranged chronologically; Movie

Materials: Playbills, Posters, and Campaign Books,
listed chronologically; Several Recordings; and an Ad-
denda section. Each item has descriptive notes and
there are a number of photographs of various items
located at various places throughout the catalog.

1. Bibliography. 2. Book Collecting. 3. Campaign
Books. 4. Catalogs, Booksellers'. 5. First Editions.
6. Phonorecords. 7. Playbills. 8. Posters.

137. Modern Language Association of America. MLA International Bibliography of Books and Articles on the Modern
Languages and Literatures. New York: The Association,
1921- .
    Well known for its comprehensiveness, this work is
possibly the most authoritative source for books and
articles relating to all modern languages and literatures.
The title, scope, and method of publication have varied.
From 1922-1969 the bibliographies were published annually in the June issue of PMLA (Publications of the
Modern Language Association of America). The bibliographies for 1921-1955 were titled "American Bibliography" and included only American scholarship.
The bibliographies for 1956-1962 were titled "Annual
Bibliography" and gradually became more international
in scope and coverage. From 1969 to 1980 it consisted
of three volumes bound in one. This was expanded to
five volumes in one with the enhanced version beginning
in 1981. The present structure is as follows: Volume
I, British, American, Australian, English-Canadian, New
Zealand, and English-Caribbean literatures; Volume II,
European, Asian, African, and South American Literatures; Volume III, Linguistics; Volume IV, General
Literature and Related Topics; and Volume V, Folklore.
    Currently the arrangement is classified, particularly
for Volume I, where you will look for materials relating
to John Steinbeck. Within the geographical area of
"American Literature" there is a breakdown by general
categories such as "Autobiography," "Fiction," and then
by chronological period such as "American Literature/
1900-1999." Following some more general categories,
materials about various writers are arranged alphabetically by surname. Under each author's name the
entries are arranged by genre, such as "Bibliography,"

"Fiction," "Fiction (name of a particular work and the
date)," and "Novel/(name of the novel and the date it
was published)." At the conclusion of this volume
there is a "Document Author Index." This index contains the names of all document authors, editors, il-
lustrators, translators, etc., represented in the classified sequence. The name of the author, editor and
so on is listed first, followed by the volume number
and entry number for the document listed. Volume
and entry numbers appearing in parentheses indicate
that the item number listed directly before the parentheses was listed in two or more volumes. There is a
second separate volume to the annual bibliography containing a subject index to Volumes I-V. This index al-
lows the researcher to find materials by theme or secondary authors or topics not evident from the citation's
place in the classified scheme. In searching for materials related to John Steinbeck look first in the classified section in the main volume under "American
Literature/1900-1999" and then alphabetically under
his name. Also check under his name in the Subject
Index volume for additional materials in other classified
sections.

Online Version: The DIALOG system (File 71) carries the MLA database from 1970 to the present. The
database does contain a coding scheme that provides a
convenient method of selecting large national and
chronological groups as well as individual authors.

1. Criticism and Interpretation.

138.   Monteiro, Stephen. "Steinbeck in Translation." Steinbeck Quarterly, 17 (Summer-Fall 1984), 103-104.
        Referring to the Goldstone/Payne bibliography:
John Steinbeck: A Bibliographical Catalogue of the
Adrian H. Goldstone Collection, published in 1974 as
the definitive bibliography of Steinbeck's works,
Monteiro, in this brief bibliographical article, adds
some titles to Seciton D of Goldstone/Payne which lists
foreign translations. Five titles are added to the
Portuguese section and one to the Spanish section.

1. Translations.   2. Translations, Portuguese.   3.
Translations, Spanish.

139. Moore, Harry Thornton. The Novels of John Steinbeck:
A First Critical Study. Chicago: Normandie House, 1939.
102p. 2nd ed. With a contemporary epilogue. Port Washington, N.Y.: Kennikat Press, 1968. 106p.

Written shortly after The Grapes of Wrath, this pi-
oneering study provides insights into the critical atti-
tudes on the 1930s. On pages 97-100 of the 1939 edition, there is a bibliographical checklist of Steinbeck
first editions arranged chronologically. This is an attempt to describe each first edition except the play
version of Of Mice and Men. The second edition differs
somewhat from the first. The EPILOGUE on pages 97-
106, which contains some notes on Steinbeck's later
works, can possibly be considered a bibliographical essay since the author discusses the materials cited.
The checklist of first editions contained in the 1939
edition is omitted.

1. Bibliography. 2. Criticism and Interpretation. 3.
First Editions.

140. Morrow (Bradford) Bookseller Ltd. John Steinbeck:
A Collection of Books and Manuscripts Formed by Harry
Valentine of Pacific Grove, California. With a foreword by
John R. Payne. Santa Barbara, CA: Bradford Morrow,
Bookseller, Ltd., 1980. 154p. (Catalogue Eight).

This compilation is an exceptionally attractive and
useful sales catalog of the collection established by
Mr. Valentine. The seven hundred numbered entries
cover a range of Steinbeck materials from manuscripts
and printed works to photographs, film posters, and
ephemera. The annotations provide excellent descriptions and frequently refer to related entries. Included
are illustrations comprising about fifty black-and-white
photographs, most quite clear, of selected items. Many
of the items described in this catalog are not found in
Goldstone/Payne.

The number of previously unrecorded items described
here along with the extensive annotations make this
catalog a valuable companion to the other major Steinbeck bibliographies published to date. Regrettably
there is no index. In terms of organization, this catalog is divided into nine main sections. Pages 9-71
list books and pamphlets by John Steinbeck in chrono-

ological sequence. Pages 73-84 list manuscripts, letters and photographs. Pages 85-98 list books with
contributions by Steinbeck. Pages 99-102 list periodical appearances by Steinbeck. Pages 103-121 list
translations of works by Steinbeck. Pages 124-130
list stage and screen materials: playscripts, playbills,
posters, campaign books, and screenplays. Pages 131-
142 list books, pamphlets, bibliographies, periodical
articles, and other secondary materials about Steinbeck.
Pages 143-149 list books from the library of John
Steinbeck. Finally, pages 151-154 list recordings and
miscellaneous items.

1. Bibliographies. 2. Bibliography. 3. Blurbs. 4.
Books and Reading. 5. Campaign Books. 6. Catalogs,
Booksellers'. 7. Correspondence. 8. Criticism and
Interpretation. 9. Ephemera. 10. First Editions. 11.
Manuscripts. 12. Misattributed Works. 13. Moving-
Picture Plays. 14. Phonorecordings. 15. Phonotapes.
16. Photographs. 17. Playbills. 18. Posters. 19.
Ricketts, Edward Flanders, 1896-1948. 20. Sources.
21. Study and Teaching--Outlines, Syllabi, etc. 22.
Translations.

141.   Myers, Robin, ed. <u>A Dictionary of Literature in the</u>
<u>English Language, From Chaucer to 1940.</u> New York: Per-
gamon Press, 1970-1971. 2v.
       This work contains bio-bibliographies of about 3,500
authors. Arrangement is alphabetical by author, with
cross references for pseudonyms. Volume 2 is a title
index. Material by and about Steinbeck is found on
page 808 of Volume 1. Following a very brief biographical sketch there is a checklist of two bibliographical
items, then a checklist of novels and short stories,
followed by a checklist of other related works. All of
these checklists have items arranged chronologically.

1. Bibliography. 2. Biography. 3. Criticism and Interpretation.

142.   Nakayama, Kayoshi. "Steinbeck Criticism in Japan:
1976-1977." <u>Steinbeck Quarterly</u>, 12 (Summer-Fall 1979),
115-122.

This bibliographical essay extends to several others
covering articles and other critical materials published
in Japan during 1976-77.

1. Criticism and Interpretation--Japan.

143. The National Union Catalog. Washington, D.C.: Library of Congress, 1953- . V. 1- .
        The printed catalogs of great libraries are invaluable
bibliographical aids to the scholar. Their catalogs are
the nearest approach to universal bibliography in the
world today. They are indispensable in verifying and
locating items. Of these perhaps the most useful catalog is that of the Library of Congress, founded in 1800.
Since 1870 the Library of Congress has received for
deposit a copy of all works copyrighted in the United
States and acquired significant books from throughout
the world. Although there is coverage prior to 1953,
it was in this year that this publication became The
National Union Catalog thus listing works contributed
by other libraries and listing locations. This catalog
is an author listing only. In 1950 the Library of
Congress began issuing The Subject Catalog, the ful-
lest and most up-to-date subject catalog for modern
books. This work is perhaps the most extensive source
for you to identify book-length Steinbeck works in most
of their varied editions including foreign translations.
There are several cumulations of this important set.
The first is The National Union Catalog Pre-1956 Imprints. London: Mansell Publishing, 1967-1981.
754v. Another important cumulated set is, The National Union Catalog ... 1956 through 1967. Totowa,
N.J.: Rowman and Littlefield, 1970-1972. 125v. Up
to 1982 the Library of Congress issued two other cumulated sets, the first covering 1968-1972 and the second
1973-1977. From 1978 to 1982 only annual cumulations
have been issued. Since 1983 the National Union Catalog has been published annually only in a microfiche
format which makes it difficult to use unless you have
access to a microfiche reader and/or printer.

1. Bibliography. 2. Translations.

144. Nevius, Blake, comp. The American Novel, Sinclair
Lewis to the Present. Northbrook, IL: AHM Publishing
Corp., 1970. 126p.
    This is a highly classified list of primary and sec-
ondary material including listings for 48 individual
novelists. Some brief critical annotations of the secondary material is provided. There is an Author/Sub-
ject Index. The bibliography on pages 87-90 lists
several articles by Steinbeck along with books and
articles about him. This bibliography covers bibliographies, biographical and critical books, biographical and critical essays.

    1. Bibliographies. 2. Bibliography. 3. Biography.
    4. Criticism and Interpretation.

144a. New York Times Index. New York: New York Times
Company, 1851-1906 and 1912- . V. 1- .
    Considered by many as a major reference source for
an accurate chronological list of important events. Published semi-monthly with quarterly and annual cumulations since 1930, this publication presents an extensive
and detailed look into the world news as reported by
the New York Times. It cites the date, page, and
column, with many cross references, and serves as a
reference for material in other newspapers as well.
One of the features that you will find most attractive
is the brief synopsis under each entry, which frequently
makes references to the newspaper itself unnecessary.
Since 1939 this index has listed a fair number of articles
about John Steinbeck and his family.

    1. Newspapers--Indexes. 2. New York Times--Indexes.

145. Nilon, Charles H. Bibliography of Bibliographies In
American Literature. New York: Bowker, 1970. 483p.
    Begun as an attempt to ascertain the quantity of bib-
liography that had been produced in American literature
and some sense of the varieties of bibliographic forms
that are in common use, this work lists over 6,400 author bibliographies. Within all of the sections of this
bibliography entries are arranged alphabetically by
authors' names. There are two exceptions. Those are

the first two sections of Part One: Bibliography.
Section 1, Basic American Bibliography, is arranged
chronologically, according to historical time periods
covered by works cited. Section 2, Library of Congress
and National Union Catalogs, is arranged chronologically
within four topical areas comprised by Library of Congress and National Union materials: authors, imprints,
subjects, and manuscript collections. Ten bibliographies
are listed under John Steinbeck on pages 244-245.
There is an extensive author and title index. (See
also: 74).

1. Bibliographies.

146. O'Connor, Richard. John Steinbeck. New York:
McGraw-Hill, 1970. 121p.
        This work is intended to be a critical overview of
Steinbeck's career written for young people. There is
a chronological list of Steinbeck's books found on pages
124-125. On page 126 there is a brief bibliography of
eight books about Steinbeck and his times. This list
includes one article by Steinbeck which he wrote for the
New York Times in 1953.

1. Bibliography. 2. Criticism and Interpretation.

147. Owens, Louis D. John Steinbeck's Re-vision of America.
Athens, GA: University of Georgia Press, 1985. 225p.
        Professor Owens examines how Steinbeck used his
concept of America to explore the moral bankruptcy of
American society, to expose the corruption that lay beneath the beckoning surface of the American dream.
There are two separate sections in this work of a bibliographical nature. The first is a "Note on Editions
Cited" on page xiii which is a chronological list of Steinbeck titles from Cup of Gold (1929) to Steinbeck: A
Life in Letters (1975). The seocnd is the "Notes" to
various chapters on pages 211-222 arranged in order of
their use in the text.

1. Bibliography. 2. Criticism and Interpretation.

147a. Owens, Louis Dean. "A New Eye in the West: Steinbeck's California Fiction." Ph.D. Dissertation. Davis: University of California at Davis, 1981. 307 leaves.
     Doctoral dissertations like master's theses and re-
search papers are excellent tools for finding bibliographic sources leading to needed information. This
dissertation is a particularly good example with a
selected bibliography on leaves 298-307. These sources
are especially useful because they lead to much related
material that would be difficult to locate otherwise. As
a genre doctoral dissertations are generally more available than master's theses and are covered well bibliographically. (See: Dissertations Abstracts International, 47)

     1. Bibliography.   2. Criticism and Interpretation.

148. Petersen, Carol. John Steinbeck. 2nd ed. Berlin:
Colloquium Verlag, 1975. 93p. (Kopfe des XX. Jahrhunderts, V. 70).
     This work, published in German, provides the
European reader with a well-conceived introduction to
Steinbeck's life and writing. A brief bibliography of
works about Steinbeck appears on page 91. A chronological list of works by Steinbeck is included on
pages 92-93.

     1. Bibliography.   2. Criticism and Interpretation.

149. Pitts, Dana. "A Descriptive Bibliography of Part of
the Steinbeck Collection at California State University, San
Jose." An MA Research Paper. San Jose, CA: Dept. of
Librarianship, California State University, San Jose, May
1973. 32 leaves.
     This unpublished research paper is a descriptive
bibliography that includes items located in the Steinbeck Research Center at San Jose State University.
The Steinbeck editions described include: Burning
Bright, In Dubious Battle, Of Mice and Men (both the
novel and the play), The Moon Is Down (both the
novel and the play), The Short Reign of Pippin IV,
and The Wayward Bus. The method of bibliographic
description follows the standards established for

bibliographies of this kind and are discussed in detail
in the introduction.

1. Burning Bright.   2. In Dubious Battle.   3. Of Mice
and Men.   4. Of Mice and Men (Play).   5. The Moon
Is Down.   6. The Moon Is Down (Play).   7. The Short
Reign of Pippin IV.   8. The Wayward Bus.

150.   Play Index: An Index to Plays.   New York: H. W.
Wilson Co., 1953- .
  Supplements for this indexing service are published
irregularly.   It contains author entries with facts
about the play -- a one-sentence summary, number of
men and women characters, and scene location.   For
plays by Steinbeck simply look under his name in the
main volume and supplements.

1. Plays--Indexes.

151.   Powell, Lawrence Clark.   "John (Ernst) Steinbeck,
1902- ."   Publishers' Weekly, 131 (April 17, 1937), 1701.
  This is a chronological list of Steinbeck's first
seven works including two additional items.   Along
with the bibliographical data there are notes containing
publication information.   This article was part of a
Publishers' Weekly series entitled "American First Editions," edited by Jacob Blanck.

1. Bibliography.   2. Book Collecting.   3. First Editions.

152.   Powell, Lawrence Clark.   "Toward a Bibliography of
John Steinbeck."   Colophon, New Series, No. 4 (Autumn
1938), 558-568.
  Powell discusses, in this largely bibliographical essay, his experiences in collecting Steinbeck early editions.   Along the way he provides some valuable publication information on these early editions not available
elsewhere before the publication of this article.   At
the conclusion is a "Check List of First Editions" up to
1938, arranged in chronological order with additional
publication information.   This article is very useful for
those interested in the historical development of
Steinbeck's early works.

1. Bibliography.   2. Book Collecting.   3. First Editions.

153.   Pownhall, David E.   Articles on Twentieth Century
Literature: An Annotated Bibliography, 1954-1970.   New
York: Kraus-Thomson Organization, 1973-1980.   7v.
       This compilation is based on but not limited to the
annotated bibliographies appearing in the journal
Twentieth Century Literature.   It includes scholarly
and critical articles, but not reviews.   There are two
major divisions in this work: (1) articles on authors
as subjects (arranged with general articles on the
author first, then articles on individual works), and
(2) general literary topics (arranged around subject
headings listed in the front matter of the final volume).
The annotations are in the form of brief abstracts.
An annotated list of articles by and about Steinbeck is
found in Volume 6, pages 4014-4037, items S1908-S2020.
Items S1908-S1953 are arranged by author and cover
critical articles about Steinbeck and four that he wrote
himself.   Items S1954-S2020 include articles about
specific Steinbeck works that are arranged in alphabetical sequence by title.

1. Bibliography.   2. Criticism and Interpretation.

154.   Pratt, John Clark.   John Steinbeck: A Critical Essay.
Grand Rapids, MI: William B. Eerdmans Publisher, 1970.
48p.   (Contemporary Writers in Christian Perspective).
       In this pamphlet, Pratt discusses Steinbeck's use of
Christian elements in "syncretic allegories."   The
selected bibliography is located on pages 46-48.   It includes one bibliography, one biographical source, a
chronological list of fifteen Steinbeck titles, and a
checklist of materials about Steinbeck including books,
and critical articles, all arranged alphabeticlly by
author.

1. Bibliographies.   2. Bibliography.   3. Biography.
4. Criticism and Interpretation.

155.   The Reader's Adviser: A Layman's Guide to Literature.

12th ed.   Edited by Sarah L. Prakken.   New York: Bowker,
1974.   3v.
    Designed primarily for the bookseller and librarian,
however, this work is useful for almost everyone interested in good reading.   Steinbeck is treated in Volume
1, on pages 587-589.   Following a biographical sketch
there is a checklist of Steinbeck works available mostly
in paperback editions.   Prices are also given.   This is
followed by a checklist of books about Steinbeck.

    1. Bibliography.   2. Biography.   3. Criticism and In-
terpretation.

156.   Readers' Guide to Periodical Literature.   New York:
H. W. Wilson Company, 1905- . V. 1- .
    This well-known author and subject index of the
more general and popular literature contains an extensive number of citations relating to Steinbeck, beginning
with Volume 9 (July 1932-June 1935).   Consult the
various volumes or issues under Steinbeck's name to
find articles.   (See also: 128)

    1. Biography--Indexes.   2. Criticism and Interpreta-
tion--Periodicals--Indexes.

157.   Reimann, Solveig.   John Steinbeck: Realist og Ro-
mantiker.   Koberhavn, Denmark: Gronbechs Forlag, 1961.
96p.
    This is a comparative study of Steinbeck as a realist
or romanticist, published in the Danish language.   The
bibliography on pages 94-96 is broken down into five
sections: works by Steinbeck, Danish translations,
Norwegian translations, Swedish translations, and works
about Steinbeck.   The items cited in each of these
lists are chronologically arranged.

    1. Bibliography.   2. Criticism and Interpretation.   3.
Translations, Danish.   4. Translations, Norwegian.
5. Translations, Swedish.

158.   Remords, Georges.   "John Steinbeck--Note Bibliograph-
ique."   Strausbourg, Université--Faculté des Lettres--Bulle-

<u>tin</u>. 28 (April 1950), 301-305.

This bibliography lists both works by and about
Steinbeck. Section I is a chronological listing of English and American editions. Section II lists French
translations and foreign editions. Section III is a list
of critical studies including books and articles in
French and English.

1. Bibliography. 2. Criticism and Interpretation.
3. Translations, French. 4. Translations.

158a. <u>Research Guide to Biography and Criticism</u>. Edited
by Walton Beacham. Washington, D.C.: Research Publishing, 1985. 2v. (1362p.).

Designed to assist students in narrowing and researching topics for term papers and essay exams, this
work will also provide librarians with a tool which will
help them lead students to valuable and accessible resources. The section on John Steinbeck was written by
Joseph R. Millichap and appears on pages 1115-1118
of Volume 2. This section has seven parts arranged in
the following order: Author's Chronology, which contains some sketchy biographical information and reference to several major works; Author's Bibliography
(selected), which lists major Steinbeck titles in chronological order; Overview of Biographical Sources, which
discusses two major Steinbeck biographies; these two
sources are further evaluated in the next section entitled Evaluation of Selected Biographies; Autobiography,
which lists and briefly discusses Steinbeck's nonfictional
works; Overview of Critical Sources, which discusses the
critical response to <u>The Grapes of Wrath</u> and <u>East of
Eden</u>; and an Evaluation of Selected Criticism, which is
an annotated bibliography of eight bibliographic and
critical works related to Steinbeck studies. Because of
its evaluative comments, this work will be a very useful
starting point for the beginning student.

1. Bibliographies. 2. Bibliography. 3. Biography.
4. Criticism and Interpretation.

159. Robbins, John Albert, ed. <u>American Literary Manuscripts: A Checklist of Holdings</u> in Academic, Historical, and

Public Libraries, Museums, and Authors' Homes in the United
States. 2nd ed. Athens: University of Georgia Press,
1977. 387p.
 This work follows the basic plan of the earlier edition. It now lists some 2,800 American writers indicating, by Library of Congress symbol for nearly 600
participating libraries, the holdings of manuscripts of
creative works, journals or diaries, letters to and from
the author, special collections, etc. There is a separate list of "Authors for Whom no Holdings Were Reported." The checklist of Steinbeck manuscripts is
found on page 303. In order to understand this listing one must consult introductory pages xxvii-liii.

1. Manuscripts.

160. Rodgers, Susan J. "An Annotated Bibliography of
Criticism on John Steinbeck's The Pearl and The Wayward
Bus." An MA Research Paper. San Jose, CA: Dept. of
Librarianship, California State University, San Jose, May
1973. 67 leaves.
 The primary purpose of the author in compiling
this unpublished research paper is to aid the Steinbeck
student and scholar in the search for knowledge of
Steinbeck's meaning, techniques, and symbolism. The
body of this bibliography is divided into five chapters.
The first chapter provides introductory material and
the following three treat the novels under consideration
and doctoral dissertations written about them. Within
the chapters for each of the novels, there are separate sections for criticism in books, periodicals, book
reviews, and movie reviews. The dissertations are
arranged in a single alphabet by author. Extensive
annotations are provided for each item cited except
for those unavailable to the compiler for examination.
A discussion of sources used in the compilation of this
bibliography is contained in the introduction.

1. The Pearl--Criticism and Interpretation.   2. The
Wayward Bus--Criticism and Interpretation.

161. St. Pierre, Brian. John Steinbeck: The California
Years. San Francisco, CA: Chronicle Books, 1983. 120p.

The author attempts to chronicle Steinbeck's early
development and the influence of the California environment upon his writing. A selected bibliography of
biographical and critical works can be found on pages
116-117.

1. Biography.   2. Homes and Haunts--California.

162. Salinas Public Library. John Steinbeck, A Guide to
the Collection of the Salinas Public Library. Edited by John
Gross and Lee Richard Hayman.   Salinas, CA: The Library,
1979. 196p.
This work is a catalog of the extensive Steinbeck
collection of the Salinas Public Library. Included in
this collection is a wide range of materials from first
editions to manuscripts, correspondence, oral histories,
and the like. All of these materials are in a logical
arrangement and in detail sufficient to give the researcher a grasp of the collection's content. Designed
by John Gross, this bibliography was published in
February of 1979 in an edition of 1,000 copies, 200 of
which were numbered in a limited edition. In terms of
organization, this guide is arranged into sixteen major
sections. The first section lists John Steinbeck's separately published works. Entries are arranged chronologically by the first date of publication. The title of
the book, place of publication, publisher, and date are
provided, followed by a brief statement about each book.
Editions are then listed with cross references to the
Goldstone/Payne Catalogue. Those editions with dust
jackets (DJ) are noted, as are paperback editions (PB).
A number of illustrations and page reproductions are
interspersed throughout this section.
In the second section, Steinbeck's contributions to
books are listed in chronological order. The citations
include original contributions, such as prefaces, introductions, and material published elsewhere. Cross
references to corresponding entries in the Goldstone/
Payne Catalogue are provided. When the notation
[Copy] is given, this indicates a xerographic copy of
the material is cited rather than the book itself. Articles by Steinbeck appearing in the periodical literature
are listed in the third section. Both original and previously published materials are listed in chronological

order. Cross references to corresponding entries in
the Goldstone/Payne Catalogue are given. Holdings are
designated as [Copy] for xerographic or typed copies
of the articles cited, [Original] if the whole periodical
is in the collection; [Cut Original] if the article has
been clipped from the periodical. Holdings of manuscripts, galley proofs, typescripts, movie and television
scripts by and about Steinbeck are cited in Section 4.
Correspondence to and from Steinbeck is listed in Section 5. The listing is divided into three series. The
first series contains correspondence to and from Steinbeck plus a few closely related items involving his af-
fairs. Holdings in this series are itemized here and
further subdivided into original material and copies.
Series II and III list correspondence from Steinbeck
family members, friends, and acquaintances. Within
each of these sections arrangement is chronological,
with dates approximated for undated material. Section
6 covers material related to the life and works of
Steinbeck. It is subdivided into five parts. Part A,
lists books, including bibliographical and biographical
works along with literary criticisms of Steinbeck's
works. Arrangement is chronological. Part B lists
magazines and articles. It is further subdivided into
two categories: journals, biographical and critical,
and journals, reviews. Arrangement is chronological
within each part.

Additional reviews and articles, including those relating to productions of Steinbeck works, have been
clipped from magazines and filed in the Clippings
Binders and Vertical File. Programs from such productions and publicity on Steinbeck books are under
Program Announcements and Publicity Material. Part
C lists newspapers with the citations being arranged
by date of publication. Part D outlines the collection
of materials including magazine and newspaper articles
contained in the Clippings Binders. Part E discusses
the Vertical File which superseded the Binder Collections and contains all material added to the collection
after January 1, 1975. Periodical articles, book excerpts, newspaper clippings, or photocopies are included. Publicity brochures from the Steinbeck Library, Valley Guild, Chamber of Commerce, and other or-
ganizations concerning or mentioning Steinbeck are also
filed here. Theses and dissertations based upon the

life or work of Steinbeck are listed in Section 7.
Sixty-three interviews with individuals who knew John
Steinbeck and/or who knew the history of the locals
about which he wrote are described in Section 8. Cas-
sette copies and tape counterindex are available for
each interview. The citations in this list are arranged
alphabetically by the name of the interviewee.

A descriptive list of subject headings for photographs is covered in Section 9. The collection itself
consists of several hundred photographs and negatives,
mainly of Steinbeck, his family, friends, and settings
from his works. Each photograph and negative has
been numbered and described, but not in this bibliography. In Section 10, listed first are materials related
to public performances of Steinbeck's work on stage,
screen, and television. The Goldstone/Payne Catalogue
reference (e.g., GP-E4) is noted, when available, for
further information as to cast and characters. Following this listing is a short section of publicity material for Steinbeck books, and for books about him.
Memorabilia of items belonging or related to Steinbeck
are listed and described in Section 11. The entries are
in chronological sequence. Section 12 is a miscellany
of materials about Steinbeck. The items include bibliographical references, photocopies of book inscriptions,
Amnesia Glasscock poems, and other related items.
Pamphlets and articles written by and about Edward F.
Ricketts are listed in Section 13. In Section 14, there
is a chronological list of books, pamphlets, magazine
and newspaper articles about Salinas and Monterey
County history and points of interest particularly as
they relate to Steinbeck and his literary works. Listed
in Section 15 are foreign translations of Steinbeck
titles. This listing covers seventeen languages arranged
alphabetically. The English translation is provided for
each title listed. Finally, Section 16 covers phonograph
records, tape recordings, and films. These include
readings, musical compositions, and related material
based upon Steinbeck's life and published works. Regrettably there is no index to this valuable guide.

1. Archives. 2. Bibliographies. 3. Bibliography. 4.
Blurbs. 5. Correspondence. 6. Criticism and Inter-
pretation. 7. Dissertations, Academic. 8. Family. 9.
Film Adaptations--Scripts. 10. Filmscripts. 11. First

Editions. 12. Homes and Haunts. 13. Interviews.
14. Library Resources. 15. Manuscripts. 16. Memorabilia. 17. Misattributed Works. 18. Moving-Picture
Plays. 19. Phonorecords. 20. Phonotapes. 21. Photographs. 22. Program Announcements. 23. Publicity
Materials. 24. Ricketts, Edward Flanders, 1896-1948.
25. Salinas, Public Library--Catalogs. 26. Television
Adaptations--Scripts. 27. Theses, Academic. 28.
Translations.

163. Schumann, Hildegard. Zum Problem des Kritischen
Realismus bei John Steinbeck. Halle (Saale) East Germany:
Veb Max Niemeyer Verlag, 1958. 348p.
    This is a critical study of realism as used by John
    Steinbeck in his fictive works. The bibliography is
    located on pages 336-345. Section I lists works by
    Steinbeck not quite in chronological order and with
    various editions listed other than firsts. Section II
    lists materials about various Steinbeck works. Section
    III lists historical studies of literature, and Section IV
    lists works relating to the problem of realism in liter-
    ature. The latter two sections are arranged alphabeti-
    cally by author.

    1. Bibliography. 2. Criticism and Interpretation.

164. Seidel, Alison P., comp. Literary Criticism and
Authors' Biographies: An Annotated Index. Metuchen, N.J.:
Scarecrow Press, 1978. 209p.
    Indexed here are standard biographical and critical
    works, in English, generally not found in such basic
    indexes as the Biography Index or the Essay and Gen-
    eral Literature Index. The entries are organized in
    one alphabetic sequence under the writer's surname.
    Multiple entries, with book titles added, appear if the
    critical work cited discusses primarily that title. The
    annotations are brief and descriptive in nature. John
    Steinbeck is treated on pages 168-169.

    1. Biography--Indexes. 2. History and Criticism--In-
    dexes.

165. Short Story Index: An Index to Stories in Collections
and Periodicals. New York: H. W. Wilson, 1953- (Supplements published irregularly).
        This work indexes tens of thousands of short
        stories that are published in anthologies and other col-
        lections. The author, title, and subject index facili-
        tates search, for it provides a ready-made author bib-
        liography. Supplements provide current information on
        recently published anthologies. In the back of the
        book is a list of indexed collections. For the collections
        which contain short stories by John Steinbeck, simply
        look under his name and then check the list in the back
        of the main volume or supplement.

        1. Short Stories--Indexes.

166. Siefker, Donald L. "Steinbeck and Best Sellers."
Steinbeck Quarterly, 11 (Summer-Fall 1978), 106-107.
        In this article, Mr. Siefker analyzes the best sellers
        among the Steinbeck canon as revealed in Alice Payne
        Hackett's 80 Years of Best Sellers, 1895-1975 (New
        York: Bowker, 1977). This discussion shows that
        Steinbeck has done well with respect to other American
        writers.

        1. Best Sellers. 2. Bibliography.

167. Simmonds, Roy S. "The First Publication of Steinbeck's
      'The Leader of the People'." Steinbeck Quarterly, 8
      (Winter 1975), 13-18.
        The author examines the first publication of this
        Steinbeck short story, which was first published in the
        August 1936 issue of the British magazine Argosy. He
        also lists 125 variants and analyzes their relationship to
        the American and British appearances.

        1. "The Leader of the People" (Short Story). 2. Short
        Stories.

168. Simmonds, Roy S. "John Steinbeck: Works Published
in the British Magazine Argosy." Steinbeck Quarterly, 4
(Fall 1971), 101-105.

The author points out in his introduction that it is
important to be aware that the British magazine <u>Argosy</u>
marked the first appearance of several Steinbeck works.
A detailed checklist of these works is provided in chronological order accompanied by extensive notes.

1. Bibliography.   2. Short Stories.

169.   Simmonds, Roy S.   "John Steinbeck's World War II Dispatches: An Annotated Checklist."   <u>Serif</u>, 11 (Summer 1974),
21-30.
This checklist comprises those dispatches written by
Steinbeck for the <u>New York Herald Tribune</u>.   These
dispatches were widely syndicated in the United States
and several of them also appeared at the same time in the
British national newspaper the <u>Daily Express</u>.   Simmonds
limits himself to the dispatches appearing in these two
newspapers.   The checklist itself contains eighty-five
entries arranged in chronological sequence.   Under
each dispatch is listed the several places it appeared.
These sources are identified by an abbreviation list
just preceding the checklist.   Notes are provided on
some of the dispatches for clarification.

1. World War, 1939-1945--Dispatches.

170.   Simmonds, Roy S.   "The Original Manuscripts of
Steinbeck's 'The Chrysanthemums.'"   <u>Steinbeck Quarterly</u>, 7
(Summer-Fall 1974), 102-111.
In this article, Mr. Simmonds provides some valuable
insights about the two original manuscripts of this much
discussed Steinbeck short story.   This article may be
of particular value or interest to textual bibliographers
for the detailed bibliographical information it contains.

1. "The Chrysanthemums" (Short Story)--Manuscripts.

171.   Simmonds, Roy S.   <u>Steinbeck's Literary Achievement</u>.
Muncie, IN: John Steinbeck Society of America, English
Dept., Ball State University, 1976.   40p.   (Steinbeck Mono-
graph Series, No. 6).
In this assessment of Steinbeck, the author attempts

to balance two opposite views and put them into proper
perspective. Although there is no bibliography per se
in this monograph, there is a rich amount of bibliographical information contained in the notes which accompany the text.

1. Criticism and Interpretation.

172. Simmonds, Roy S. "Steinbeck's 'The Murder': A Critical and Bibliographical Study." Steinbeck Quarterly, 9
(Spring 1976), 45-53.
      Mr. Simmonds provides a careful textual study of
this particular short story which was Steinbeck's first
to be published in a British magazine. Along with other
bibliographical data, the author in an appendix lists the
variants between the Viking text and the North American Review and Lovat Dickinson's Magazine texts.

1. "The Murder" (Short Story)--Criticism and Interpretation.

173. Simmonds, Roy S. "The Typescript of Steinbeck's
America and Americans." Steinbeck Quarterly, 4 (Fall 1971),
120-121.
      The author details his examination of this typescript
and recalls some of the pertinent bibliographical details
since he was not able to take notes at the time. A
description of this typescript from the Southeby & Company sale catalogue is reprinted here.

1. America and Americans. 2. First Editions.

174. Sixteen Modern American Authors: A Survey of Research and Criticism. Edited by Jackson R. Bryer. Revised
edition. New York: Norton, 1973. 673p. (The Norton Library).
      In this compilation a number of specialists present
surveys of the published editions, critical studies, biographies, and available manuscripts and letters of sixteen twentieth-century authors, all of whom are now
dead. The chapter on Steinbeck (pages 499-527) was
written by Warren French. It is in the form of a bib-

liographical essay and is divided into five major sections plus a supplement. Section I is a bibliography
of bibliographies; Section II, covers basic editions of
major works; Section III discusses manuscripts and
letters; Section IV deals with biographical sources; and
Section V lists and discusses critical works. This section is further divided into parts covering books, articles and parts of books, individual works, and Steinbeck's foreign reputation. The supplement is arranged,
for the most part, like the main part of the chapter.
Because of the annotations, this is a very useful bibliographic instrument for the Steinbeck student.

1. Bibliographies. 2. Bibliography. 3. Biography.
4. Correspondence. 5. History and Criticism. 6.
Manuscripts.

175. Social Sciences Citation Index. Philadelphia, PA: Institute for Scientific Information, 1973- . V. 1-
     The organization and purpose of this citation index-
ing service are exactly the same as for the Arts & Humanities Citation Index (see 8). There are a number
of Steinbeck related items to be found here. Online
Version: Social Scisearch (File 7) is the online version
of the printed citation indexes but extends the database by including more journals in other disciplines
and is available on the DIALOG system. The database
is updated monthly and is searchable by title of work,
source authors, journal names, corporate source, and
cited references. A number of Steinbeck related items
continue to turn up here that would be difficult to locate otherwise.

1. Criticism and Interpretation--Citation Indexes.

176. Sociological Abstracts. San Diego, CA: Sociological
Abstracts, 1953- . V. 1-
     Of the many indexing and abstracting services avail-
able to the student this is one of the more difficult to
use. Issued six times per year it provides approximately 7,000 abstracts each year to materials related to so-
ciology. Materials abstracted include periodical articles,
conference papers, and the like. Abstracts are ar-

ranged in classified (subject) order in 28 major categories with numerous subdivisions. Separate author
and subject indexes are included in each issue and cumulated subject indexes that are published a few months
after the last issue of each volume. An index covering
1943-1962 and one covering 1963-1967 have been published for this set. To find items related to John
Steinbeck look in the Subject Index. There are a number of items listed in this source. Online Version:
Sociological Abstracts (File, 37) is also available on the
DIALOG system from 1963 to the present. This
machine-readable database is updated quarterly and is
a valuable source for Steinbeck related materials you
might not find otherwise.

1. History and Criticism--Abstracts.

177. Stanford University. Libraries. A Catalogue of the
John Steinbeck Collection at Stanford University. Compiled
and edited by Susan F. Riggs; with an introduction by
Jackson J. Benson. Stanford, CA: Stanford University Libraries, 1980. 194p.
      This catalog is a comprehensive listing of Stanford's
extensive Steinbeck collection, housed in the Department of Special Collections. Its primary emphasis is on
Steinbeck's letters, of which there are more than a
thousand, many of them unpublished and some previously unknown. Also itemized are many manuscripts,
books, and memorabilia. The body of this work is
divided into fourteen major sections. The first section
lists letters and documents written by Steinbeck arranged alphabetically by recipient. Section 2, lists letters to Steinbeck arranged alphabetically by writer.
Letters relating to Steinbeck are listed in Section 3,
and are arranged alphabetically by writer. Section 4,
lists manuscripts, and typescripts of major pieces, arranged by approximate date. Proofs of books are
listed in section 5, and are arranged chronologically.
      Section 6, lists books and separately published short
pieces including translations arranged in chronological
sequence. Steinbeck's contributions to other books are
listed in Section 7. This listing is arranged by the
date of each book's publication. Section 8, lists contributions to periodicals, arranged by the date of each

periodical's publication. Screen plays and published
work based on Steinbeck's fiction are listed in Section
9. The entries in this section are arranged by the
date of the adaptation or publication. Section 10 lists
miscellanea including manuscripts and typescripts of
minor pieces, tearsheets and photocopies of Steinbeck
pieces, reviews and articles about Steinbeck, press
coverage of Steinbeck's travels, memorabilia, photographs and artwork, related items, recordings, and
filmstrips.

Works misattributed to Steinbeck are listed in Section 11. Eight bibliographies are listed in Section 12.
Section 13 has a selected list of books and journals
relating to Steinbeck arranged by date of publication.
Section 14 is a selected list of articles and pamphlets
about and relating to Steinbeck arranged by date.
This work has an index to letters, documents, and major manuscripts. It will be of immense value to the
student, collector, or literary critic who wishes to
pursue themes in Steinbeck's thinking, or certain events
in his life. The introduction was written by Jackson J.
Benson, a prominent Steinbeck authority and his offi-
cial biographer.

1. Bibliographies. 2. Bibliography. 3. Correspondence.
4. Criticism and Interpretation. 5. Film Adaptations--
Scripts. 6. Filmstrips. 7. Homes and Haunts. 8.
Manuscripts. 9. Memorabilia. 10. Misattributed Works.
11. Phonorecords. 12. Phonotapes. 13. Photographs.
14. Plays. 15. Program Announcements. 16. Publicity
Materials. 17. Stanford University Libraries--Catalogs.
18. Tearsheets. 19. Translations.

178. Steele, Joan. "John Steinbeck: A Checklist of Biographical, Critical, and Bibliographical Material." Bulletin
of Bibliography, 24 (May-August 1965), 149-152. 162-163.
     The basic purpose of this bibliography is to assist
scholars interested in studying Steinbeck's work. It
covers the period 1930-1960 with a few entries for 1961
and 1962. This list contains 212 citations, and consists of books, doctoral dissertations, and essays appearing in periodicals and in published materials in the
English language. Not included are abridgments of
articles, book reviews, film reviews, or recordings.

The primary material consists solely of critical essays
written by Steinbeck which are considered to be pertinent to the dialogue between critic and author. Section I, Items 1-10 are bibliographies. Section II, Items
11-38, are biographies. Section III, Items 39-212, are
the critical materials. Each of these sections are cross-
indexed where necessary. All entries are arranged alphabetically by author and then alphabetically by title.
Articles reprinted in collections are cross-referenced by
number.

1. Bibliographies. 2. Bibliography. 3. Biography.
4. Criticism and Interpretation. 5. Dissertations, Academic.

179. Steinbeck, John. Viva Zapata! Edited by Robert E.
Morsberger. New York: Viking Press, 1975. 150p.
        The hitherto unpublished script for Viva Zapata!
was written by Steinbeck between 1948 and 1950. On
pages 145-147 there is a complete list of films written
by John Steinbeck for the screen or adapted by Steinbeck and others from his fiction. It also includes the
one film narrated by Steinbeck. The films are listed
in chronological order, with the major credits. The
bibliography on pages 149-150 contains twenty-nine
books and articles by and about Steinbeck that carry
some relationship to his films. There is also a brief
list of eight reviews of this film.

1. Film Adaptations. 2. Film Reviews. 3. Viva Zapata! (Moving Picture).

180. Steinbeck and the Arthurian Theme. Edited by Tetsumaro Hayashi. Muncie, IN: John Steinbeck Society of
America, Dept. of English, Ball State University, 1975. 48p.
(Steinbeck Monograph Series, No. 5).
        This work traces the Arthurian theme throughout
the writings of John Steinbeck. The selected bibliography is located on pages 44-46. It includes articles
and books by and about Steinbeck.

1. Arthurian Romances--History and Criticism. 2.
Bibliography. 3. Criticism and Interpretation. 4.
Sources.

181. The Steinbeck Collector. San Jose, CA: Bibliographic
Research Library, 1979- . No. 1- .
      First issued in August of 1979 this occasional news-
letter includes materials of use to book collectors interested in John Steinbeck. Much bibliographic information is provided on various Steinbeck editions along
with some auction values and a directory of Steinbeck
Specialist Booksellers.

      1. Book Collecting. 2. First Editions. 3. Periodicals.

182. Steinbeck Criticism: A Review of Book-Length Studies,
1939-1973. Edited by Tetsumaro Hayashi. Muncie, IN: John
Steinbeck Society of America, Dept. of English, Ball State
University, 1974. 48p. (Steinbeck Monograph Series, No.
4).
      This work is a collection of seventeen reviews of
book-length studies on Steinbeck published between
1939 and 1973. Along with the bibliographical information about the works reviewed, there is much bibliographical data within the body of the reviews that will
be of use to Steinbeck students.

      1. Bibliography. 2. Criticism and Interpretation.

182a. Steinbeck Newsletter (India). Jagraj Marg, India:
John Steinbeck Society of India, 1984- . No. 1- .
      Issued annually this newsletter is published by the
John Steinbeck Society of India which was founded on
December 20, 1984, as a wing of the International John
Steinbeck Society. It reports on Steinbeck related ac-
tivities and the latest research trends and publications
in India and abroad. Issues include photographs as
well as articles.

      1. Bibliography. 2. Periodicals.

183. Steinbeck Quarterly. Muncie, IN: John Steinbeck Society of America, English Dept., Ball State University, 1968-
. V. 1- .
      Formerly entitled: Steinbeck Newsletter from March
of 1968 to Vol. 2, No. 2, Summer 1969, this journal

has included articles, reviews, reports, notices, memo-
rial statements, etc., by Steinbeck students and
scholars. Most importantly it has included a great deal
of bibliographic material contributed by many different
persons under a variety of columns such as "Bibliographical Notes," "Miscellanies," and the like. This
source is especially useful for finding fugitive materials
related to Steinbeck.

1. Bibliography.   2. Periodicals.

184. Steinbeck Seminar, Taylor University, 1976. Steinbeck's
Prophetic Vision of America: Proceedings of the Taylor Uni-
versity--Ball State University Bicentennial Steinbeck Seminar
Held at Taylor University, May 1, 1976. Edited by Tetsumaro
Hayashi and Kenneth D. Swan. Upland, IN: Taylor University for the John Steinbeck Society of America, English
Dept., Ball State University, Muncie, IN, 1976. 108p.
     This is a collection of essays delivered to the Bi-
centennial Steinbeck Seminar which offer an overview
of Steinbeck's career, ranging from his fluctuating
critical reputation to his position in the stream of Mod-
ernist and Post-Modernist American literature. The
bibliography on pages 102-104 is divided into three
main sections. Section I is a checklist of Steinbeck's
major works broken down in the areas of novels, plays
and filmstrips, and nonfiction. Section II lists eighteen
books about Steinbeck. Section III lists two bibliographies.

1. Bibliographies.   2. Bibliography.   3. Criticism and
Interpretation.   4. Filmstrips.   5. Plays.

185. Steinbeck's Travel Literature: Essays in Criticism.
Edited by Tetsumaro Hayashi. Muncie, IN: John Steinbeck
Society of America, English Dept., Ball State University,
1980. 76p. (Steinbeck Monograph Series, No. 10).
     Steinbeck's travel literature has long been of inter-
est to both students and scholars alike. The eight
essays comprising this monograph were published previously in various sources. There is no formal bibliography included, however, the bibliographical notes
attached to each contribution contain a wealth of useful

information and direction in this area of Steinbeck
studies.

1. Criticism and Interpretation.   2. Voyages and
Travels.

186. Steinbeck's Women: Essays in Criticism. Edited by
Tetsumaro Hayashi. Muncie, IN: John Steinbeck Society
of America, English Dept., Ball State University, 1979. 54p.
(Steinbeck Monograph Series, No. 9).
This work is a collection of six critical essays on
Steinbeck's attention to the fictional female and pre-
sents many questions and suggests several conclusions.
The selected bibliography on pages 53-54 lists seventeen
critical studies. Entries arranged alphabetically by
author.

1. Characters--Women.   2. Criticism and Interpretation.

187. A Study Guide to Steinbeck's "The Long Valley."
Edited by Tetsumaro Hayashi. Ann Arbor, MI: Pierian
Press, 1976. 140p.
This compendium consists of a collection of fifteen
critical essays corresponding to the exact number and
order of stories in the Viking Press edition of The Long
Valley (1938). Brian Barbour concludes this collection
with a sixteenth essay in which he assesses Steinbeck's
contribution to the short story genre as a whole. A
special feature of this work is that each essay, except
for the concluding one, is accompanied by five pertinent discussion questions which provide excellent
stimuli for independent thought or, in classroom situa-
tions, for discussion or term paper topics. On pages
133-136 is a selected checklist of books and articles
relating to this particular steinbeck work. Several of
these are briefly annotated.

1. Criticism and Interpretation.   2. The Long Valley--
Study and Teaching--Outlines, Syllabi, etc.

188. Syracuse, N.Y. Public Library. Gold Star List of
American Fiction. Fiftieth Anniversary Edition. Syracuse,

N.Y.: The Library, 1966. 78p.
 This work is a basic list of fiction by American
authors of note. Page 36 includes a list of six Steinbeck titles arranged in alphabetical order. For each
title there is listed the date of first appearance along
with a brief synopsis of the work.

 1. Bibliography.

189. Texas. University. Humanities Research Center.
John Steinbeck: An Exhibition of American and Foreign
Editions. Austin, Texas: The Center, 1963. 31p.
 This exhibition catalogue lists thirty-six of Steinbeck's major works published through 1962. The works
are arranged chronologically. Full bibliographical data
is given for first and subsequent editions along with
extensive notes in some cases. Also provided are illustrations of jacket covers for foreign language editions and several other items of interest. Item No. 36
lists five Steinbeck anthologies. This catalogue is a
useful supplement to the Goldstone/Payne Catalogue
(67) particularly for its listing of foreign language editions. Two thousand copies of this catalogue were published. It was designed by Cyril Datorsky and the introduction written by William B. Todd.

 1. Bibliography. 2. Exhibition Catalogs. 3. First
 Editions. 4. Translations.

190. Thompson, Robert J. "A Survey of Recent John Steinbeck Criticism and a Partial Bibliography of the San Jose
State College Library Steinbeck Collection." An MA Research
Paper. San Jose, CA: Dept. of Librarianship, San Jose
State College, June 1972. 37 leaves.
 This unpublished research paper was compiled to
assist those using the Steinbeck collection at San Jose
State College (now San Jose State University). Chapter
1 is a survey discussion of Steinbeck criticism up to
1971 which culminates with a list of works cited. The
partial bibliography of works in the Steinbeck collection
at San Jose State contained in Chapter 2 is broken down
into the categories of novels, contributions, collected
works, criticism, magazine articles and stories by Stein-

beck, magazine articles about Steinbeck, and a miscellany section. Some entries contain descriptive matter
especially if a particular work has an inscription or is
signed and some others are briefly annotated.

1. Bibliography. 2. Criticism and Interpretation.
3. Steinbeck Research Center, San Jose State Univer-
sity--Catalogs.

191. Toomey, Alice F. A World Bibliography of Bibliographies, 1964-1974.... Totowa, N.J.: Rowman and Littlefield, 1977. 2v. (xii, 1166p.).
    Compiled as a decennial supplement to the 4th edi-
tion of Theodore Besterman's A World Bibliography of
Bibliographies. This work is limited to separately
published bibliographies represented by Library of
Congress catalog cards including some offprints of bibliographies which originally appeared as part of a
larger work. Five Steinbeck bibliographies are listed
on pages 301 and 1036.

1. Bibliographies.

192. Walcutt, Charles Child, ed. Seven Novelists in the
American Naturalist Tradition: An Introduction. Minneapolis: University of Minnesota Press, 1974, c1963. 331p.
(Minnesota Library on American Writers, V. 8).
    Seven competent essays by six seasoned scholars il-
lustrate the range and diversity of naturalism's development in American literature. The essay on John Steinbeck appears on pages 205-244 and was written by
James Gray and is exactly the same as his pamphlet,
published as No. 94 by the University of Minnesota
Press in 1971. A selected bibliography is found on
pages 304-305 relating to Steinbeck. There is a chronological list of his novels, collections of short stories,
plays, and nonfiction. There is also an alphabetical
list of critical materials arranged by author.

1. Bibliography. 2. Criticism and Interpretation.

193. Walker, Warren S. Twentieth-Century Short Story

explication: Interpretations 1900-1975, of Short Fiction Since
1800. 3rd ed. Hamden, CT: Shoe String Press, Inc., 1977.
880p.
 A checklist of explicatory comment on short stories
of all countries is contained in this work. Arranged
as an author list, with short story titles given beneath
each author's name, and a checklist of explications beneath each story title. There is an index to short
story authors. Steinbeck's short stories are treated on
pages 698-702. These short stories are arranged alphabetically by title. Under each title is a number of
critical or interpretative works related to the specific
story.

 1. Short Stories--Criticism and Interpretation.

194. Walker, Warren S. Twentieth-Century Short Story Explication: Supplement I to Third Edition: With Checklists of
Books and Journals Used. Hamden, CT: Shoe String Press,
1980. 257p.
 Covers generally interpretations that have appeared
since 1900 of short stories published after 1800. In
this supplement materials cited relate to studies published from 1976-1978. Also included are items previously overlooked and recent reprints of previously
cited items. Short stories by John Steinbeck and related materials are listed on page 200.

 1. Short Stories--Criticism and Interpretation.

195. Watt, Frank William. John Steinbeck. New York:
Grove Press, Inc., 1962. 117p. (Evergreen Pilot Books,
EP 13).
 A short but knowledgeable introduction to Steinbeck
intended for European readers this work focuses on his
"regionalism" and the effect of "non-teleological thinking" on his fictive works. Watt provides a brief bibliography on pages 115-117. The first section lists
major works by Steinbeck and the second some critical
books and articles about him.

 1. Bibliography. 2. Criticism and Interpretation.

196. Wegner, Jill C. "A Survey of John Steinbeck Biography and a Partial Bibliography of the California State University, San Jose Library Steinbeck Collection." An MA Research Paper. San Jose, CA: Dept. of Librarianship, California State University, San Jose, July 1972. 43 leaves.

This unpublished research paper was prepared to assist those using the Steinbeck collection at San Jose State University in its formative years. Following a brief introduction there is a Steinbeck chronology. Chapter 1 is a bibliographic essay surveying materials in the collection broken down into the areas of novels, other works, adaptations, contributions, criticisms, articles by Steinbeck, articles about Steinbeck, and a miscellany section. All of the items in Chapter 2 are annotated. This bibliography is similar in structure to the one by Robert J. Thompson and does contain some duplication in entries but not annotations.

1. Bibliography. 2. Biography. 3. Steinbeck Research Center, San Jose State University--Catalogs.

196a. Weiner, Alan R. Literary Criticism Index. [With Spencer Means] Metuchen, N.J.: Scarecrow Press, 1984. 685p.

Designed as an index to bibliographies and checklists of literary criticism, this work attempts to provide better access to this type of information on American and British authors of note. The internal arrangement of this index is alphabetical by author. References to "General" criticism of a specific author are followed by references to criticism of the author's individual works, alphabetically arranged. Collaborative works follow the works of a single author in a new alphabetical sequence. Each entry includes a symbol or symbols and page references directing the user to appropriate volumes containing citations to critical works. You will have to consult the "Key to Symbols" for a complete bibliographic description of the source indexed. Steinbeck is treated on pages 574-575. This work is a good source for librarians to use to set patrons on the right path.

1. History and Criticism--Indexes.

196b. Weixlmann, Joe. <u>American Short-Fiction Criticism and
Scholarship</u>, 1959-1977: <u>A Checklist</u>. Athens, OH: Swallow
Press by Ohio University Press, 1982. 625p.

    Actually Weixlmann here updates previous works by
Donna L. Gerstenberger and George Hendrick (See 65,
66). The compiler scanned about 5,000 books and in-
structors' manuals, and indexes 325 serial publications,
which are listed separately and include titles with mi-
nority emphasis. Generally the work is divided into
two major parts. The first part treats general studies,
bibliographies, and other special subjects. The second
part is the larger portion of the work which treats over
five hundred authors, alphabetically arranged. Categories for each author include: short fiction titles with
relevant critical citations; general studies; interviews;
and primary and secondary bibliographies. References
cite appropriate running numbers for individual works
that are treated in more general studies. Steinbeck is
treated on pages 529-536, Items 6117-6211. This work
will be especially helpful for students and librarians
needing criticism on short fiction by Steinbeck as well
as other authors.

1. Bibliographies. 2. History and Criticism. 3. Short
Stories--History and Criticism.

197. Williams, Betty Jane. "A Descriptive Bibliography of
Four of the John Steinbeck Novels Included in the Steinbeck
Collection of the San Jose State College." An MA Research
Paper. San Jose, CA: Dept. of Librarianship, San Jose
State College, January 1972. 86 leaves.

    This unpublished research paper is a descriptive
bibliography covering the following Steinbeck works:
<u>Cannery Row</u> (1945), <u>Cup of Gold</u> (1929), <u>East of Eden</u>
(1952), and <u>The Red Pony</u> (1937). The standard rules
for descriptive bibliography are used for each edition
of the works cited. The introduction discusses the
descriptive process in some detail followed by a glos-
sary of terms. A brief bibliography of materials used
is provided on leaf 86.

1. <u>Cannery Row</u>. 2. <u>Cup of Gold</u>. 3. <u>East of Eden</u>.
4. <u>The Red Pony</u>.

198. Woodress, James Leslie. <u>American Fiction, 1900-1950:</u>
<u>A Guide to Information Sources</u>. Volume I. Detroit: Gale
Research Company, 1974. 260p. (American Literature, English Literature, and World Literatures in English: An Information Guide Series; Gale Information Guide Library).

This work is an annotated bibliographical guide to
sources of information on selected modern American fiction writers. It is arranged into two major parts:
(1) general bibliography, covering both general back-
ground and reference material and specialized source
material, and (2) a series of bibliographical essays on
44 individual authors, arranged alphabetically by name
of the author, including both primary and secondary
materials published through 1972. In section 38, pages
183-188, there is a bibliographical essay covering works
by and about Steinbeck. Following a brief biographical
sketch the essay covers bibliographies and manuscripts,
fictional works, editions and reprints, biography, and
criticism. This bibliography will be of particular interest to students because of the useful comments offered
by the compiler.

1. Bibliographies. 2. Bibliography. 3. Biography.
4. Criticism and Interpretation. 5. Manuscirpts.

199. Woodress, James Leslie. <u>Dissertations in American Lit-</u>
<u>erature, 1891-1966</u>. Newly revised and enlarged with the
assistance of Marian Koritz. Durham, N.C.: Duke University
Press, 1968. 185p.

This work is a list of 4,700 dissertations from all
countries. It is arranged as an alphabetical list of
subjects. First, individual authors as subjects are
listed, then general topics such as "Drama," "Fine
Arts," and the like. There is an author index. Items
593, 1718, and 2396-2411 are dissertations about Steinbeck arranged alphabetically by author. Each entry
lists author, title, granting institution, and date only.

1. Dissertations, Academic.

200. Woodward, Robert H. "The Steinbeck Research Center
at San Jose State University: A Descriptive Catalogue."
<u>San Jose Studies</u>, 11 (Winter 1985), 1-128.

This descriptive catalogue is intended as a selective guide to available resources located in the Steinbeck Research Center at San Jose State University. The catalogue is arranged into thirteen broad subject areas: Books by John Steinbeck, Steinbeck's Contributions to Books, Steinbeck's Contributions to Periodicals, Manuscripts and Correspondence, Books from Steinbeck's Library, Books about Steinbeck, Periodical Material about Steinbeck, Dissertations and Theses, Photographs, Audio-Visual Materials and Films, Scrapbooks and Miscellany, Edward F. Ricketts Materials, Paintings and Furnishings. The materials by Steinbeck are listed chronologically and secondary items alphabetically by author or title. Some sections within the main chapters have various logical subdivisions. The descriptive information for major Steinbeck works is extensive. There are eight photographs of Steinbeck and one of Ed Ricketts included at various places throughout the catalogue. Collectors, scholars, and students will find this work an invaluable source of information.

1. Archives. 2. Bibliographies. 3. Bibliography. 4. Blurbs. 5. Books and Reading. 6. Criticism and Interpretation. 7. Ephemera. 8. Film Adaptations. 9. First Editions. 10. Memorabilia. 11. Phonorecords. 12. Phonotapes. 13. Photographs. 14. Plays. 15. Radio Adaptations. 16. Ricketts, Edward Flanders, 1896-1947. 17. Steinbeck Research Center, San Jose State University--Catalogs. 18. Television Adaptations. 19. Translations.

201.   Workman, Brooke. <u>Writing Seminars in the Content Area: In Search of Hemingway, Salinger, and Steinbeck.</u> Urbana, IL: National Council of Teachers of English, 1983. 321p.

This work is a handbook of semester designs for classroom teachers on the high school level for seminars on Hemingway, Salinger, and Steinbeck. Part III. In Search of John Steinbeck is found on pages 217-321. A bibliography is included on pages 318-321. The materials listed in the ten divisions of this bibliography are arranged alphabetically either by author or title. The areas covered include: Basic Materials for Starting a Seminar; Valuable Books: Biography and Criticism;

Booklist: Checklist of Major Primary Sources; Scripts,
Plays, Musicals; Educational Films; Filmstrip-Record/
Cassettes; Records and Cassettes; Pictures and Posters;
and Hollywood Films.

1. Bibliography.   2. Biography.   3. Criticism and Interpretation.   4. Film Adaptations.   5. Moving-Picture
Plays.   6. Phonorecords.   7. Phonotapes.   8. Photographs.   9. Posters.   10. Study and Teaching.

202.   Zuga, Connie S.   "John Steinbeck: Sourcebook of
Articles from the <u>Monterey Peninsula Herald</u>, 1935-1968."   An
MA Research Paper.   San Jose, CA: Dept. of Librarianship,
San Jose State University, August 1974.   2v.
    This unpublished research paper was compiled with
the belief that newspaper articles provide much factual
information about Steinbeck--his life, his friends, his
opinions--as well as articles written by him.   Volume 1
of this set contains introductory material about the collection of articles plus a bibliography of sources used
or that have relevance to the project.   Of particular
interest are the appendixes.   Appendix "A" is a chronological list of issues scanned.   Appendix "B" is a
chronological list of articles giving the title and page
on which the article is found.   These are followed by
a rather general index to the articles.   The remainder
of the volume includes the articles from 1935 to 1959.
Volume II includes articles from 1960 to 1968.   The articles are arranged in chronological order with the date
marked on each page.

1. Monterey Peninsula Herald (Newspaper)--Indexes.

AUTHOR INDEX

Included in this index along with authors are editors, translators, and others connected with the works cited in this bibliography. Surnames are listed first followed by the given name and middle initials (if any); they are followed by item numbers.

Adelman, Irving 1
Allen, Robert V., tr. 120
Astro, Richard 9, 10
Auchard, John 118

Baird, Newton D. 12
Barker, David 13
Bartholet, Carolyn 117
Beacham, Walton, ed. 158a
Beebe, Maurice 14
Benson, Jackson J. 15, 177
Besterman, Theodore 16
Beyer, Preston C. 16a, 17
Blanck, Jacob 106
Bowker (R. R.) Company, New York 24
Bruccoli, Matthew J., ed. 56
Bryer, Jackson R., ed. 14, 174
Burrows, Michael 26

Callow, James T. 27
Chicorel, Marietta, ed. 28
Colby, Vineta, ed. 114
Condit, Larry D. 32
Corlett, Margaret 33
Cosby, Arlinda W. 34
Craise, Douglas L. 35

Davidson, Alice 38
Davis, Robert C., ed. 39
Davis, Robert M., ed. 40
DeMott, Robert J. 41, 42, 43, 44, 45, 46

Ditsky, John 48
Donohue, Agnes M., ed. 49
Dourgarian, James M. Bookman 49a
Dworkin, Rita 1

Ehrenhaft, George 49b
Etulain, Richard W. 52, 53

Fensch, Thomas C., ed. 54
Fenster, Valmi K. 55
Fontenrose, Joseph E. 57
Fowler, Marilyn J. 58
Frame, Louise L. 59
French, Warren G. 60, 61, 62, 119

Gannett, Lewis S. 63
Garcia, Reloy 64
Gerstenberger, Donna L. 65, 66
Gohdes, Clarence, ed. 120
Goldstone, Adrian H. 67
Gray, James 68
Greenwood, Robert 12
Gross, John, ed. 162
Gunderman, Patricia 69

Hackett, Alice P. 166
Hanson, Patricia K., ed. 129
Hanson, Stephen L., ed. 129
Harmon, Robert B. 71, 72

Included in this index are the titles of the items listed in the bibliography. Where authors, editors, etc., are connected with any of these documents just the surname is provided. Corporate entries, where appropriate, are also given. Linkage to the items is provided via the sequential numbers at the end of each title. If there are entries with the same title but different authors, they are separated by a semicolon (;).

SUBJECT INDEX

Each item in the bibliography has one or more subject
headings or descriptors assigned to it representing
subjects and/or types of materials listed bibliographically therein. Where it has been deemed necessary for
clarity, scope notes (SN) have been provided.

1, 16, 18, 28, 41, 44, 49, 52, 55, 56, 66, 67, 71, 72, 74, 88,
97, 111, 112, 134, 140, 144, 145, 154, 158a, 162, 174, 177, 178,
184, 191, 196b, 198, 200

BIBLIOGRAPHY
    SN: Includes works which contain bibliographies or checklists
         of materials written by Steinbeck.
    12, 13, 15, 17, 23, 31, 32, 36, 40, 41, 44, 49, 49a, 49b, 50, 54,
    55, 56, 57, 62, 63, 67, 68, 70, 71, 73, 77, 80, 84, 86, 87, 88,
    89, 90, 93, 104, 105, 108, 109a, 110, 113, 114, 119, 121, 122,
    123, 124, 125, 126, 130, 134, 135, 136, 139, 140, 141, 143, 144,
    146, 147, 147a, 148, 151, 152, 153, 154, 155, 157, 158, 158a,
    162, 163, 166, 168, 174, 177, 178, 180, 181, 182, 182a, 183, 184,
    189, 190, 192, 195, 196, 198, 200, 201
    Rare Books   3

BIOGRAPHY   2, 10, 11, 15, 24, 27, 33, 54, 55, 63, 84, 97, 109a,
    112, 113, 114, 134, 141, 144, 154, 155, 158a, 161, 174, 178, 188,
    196, 198, 201
    Indexes   19, 75, 76, 156, 164

BLURBS
    SN: Works cited below include lists of materials carrying short
         publicity notices (as on dust jacket) by Steinbeck.
    67, 140, 162, 200

BOOK COLLECTING   13, 17, 49a, 56, 70, 71, 106, 136, 151, 152,
    181

BOOK REVIEWS   12, 83, 87, 88
    Indexes   20, 21, 29, 31, 37, 100

BOOKS
    Prices   3, 22, 23

BOOKS AND READING
    SN: Citations refer to books owned or read by Steinbeck.
    46, 140, 200

BURNING BRIGHT   149
    Criticism and Interpretation   93

CAMPAIGN BOOKS
    SN: Here are cited materials related to a planned set of promo-
         tional activities, including advertising and publicity usual-
         ly for Steinbeck film adaptations.
    136, 140

CANNERY ROW   197
    Criticism and Interpretation   34, 93

IN DUBIOUS BATTLE   149
    Criticism and Interpretation   93, 131

INTERVIEWS   162

LAWRENCE, DAVID HERBERT (1885-1930)   64

"THE LEADER OF THE PEOPLE" (short story)   167

LIBRARY
    Catalogs   46

LIBRARY RESOURCES
    70, 90, 162

THE LOG FROM THE SEA OF CORTEZ
    Criticism and Interpretation   93

THE LONG VALLEY
    Criticism and Interpretation   59, 93
    Study and Teaching
          Outlines, Syllabi, Etc.   187

LOS ANGELES TIMES (newspaper)
    Indexes   108

MANUSCRIPTS
    83, 87, 88, 140, 159, 162, 174, 177, 198
    Prices   3

MEMORABILIA
    SN: Here are works containing lists of things that are remark-
         able and worthy of remembrance such as the Nobel Prize
         medal, Pigasus stamp, and the like.
    162, 177, 200

MISATTRIBUTED WORKS
    140, 162, 177

MISCELLANIES, NON-FICTION   58

MONTEREY PENINSULA HERALD (newspaper)
    Indexes   108, 202

THE MOON IS DOWN   149
    Criticism and Interpretation   35, 93

THE MOON IS DOWN (moving picture)
    Criticism and Interpretation   35

THE MOON IS DOWN (play)   149

PLAYS
    67, 83, 87, 88, 122, 177, 184, 200
    Indexes 7, 150

PLOTS
    Indexes 110

POETRY 83, 87, 88

POSTERS 49a, 136, 140, 201

PROGRAM ANNOUNCEMENTS 162, 177

RADIO ADAPTATIONS 67, 200

THE RED PONY 197
    Criticism and Interpretation 131

REGISTER-PAJARONIAN [WATSONVILLE] (newspaper)
    Indexes 108

RICKETTS, EDWARD FLANDERS (1896-1948)
    9, 10, 52, 140, 162, 200

A RUSSIAN JOURNAL
    Criticism and Interpretation 93

SALINAS CALIFORNIAN (newspaper)
    Indexes 33, 108

SALINAS DAILY INDEX (newspaper)
    Indexes 33

SALINAS INDEX-JOURNAL (newspaper)
    Indexes 33, 108

SALINAS PUBLIC LIBRARY
    Catalogs 162

SALINAS PUBLIC LIBRARY
    Non-Book Materials
        Indexes 108

SAN FRANCISCO CHRONICLE (newspaper)
    Indexes 108

SAN FRANCISCO EXAMINER (newspaper)
    Indexes 108

SAN JOSE MERCURY NEWS (newspaper)
    Indexes 108

SERIES INDEX

Some of the items cited in the bibliography are parts of numbered
or unnumbered series. These may be important to researchers who
are interested in sources related to those that deal specifically with
John Steinbeck. All of the items related to a specific series are
listed under the series entry first by series number and then alphabetically by author or title. They are linked to the annotated guide
via the sequential numbering system employed in the other indexes
in this part.

GARLAND REFERENCE LIBRARY OF THE HUMANITIES, V. 246:
DeMott, Steinbeck's Reading   45

INDIANA UNIVERSITY PRESS FILMGUIDE SERIES, FG2:   French,
Filmguide to "The Grapes of Wrath"   61

KOPFE DER XX. JAHRHUNDERTS, VO. 70:   Petersen, John Steinbeck   148

MINNESOTA LIBRARY ON AMERICAN WRITERS, V. 8:   Walcutt, ed.,
Seven Novelists in the American Naturalist Tradition   192

MONOGRAPHS IN THE SCIENCES, SOCIAL SCIENCES, AND HUMANI-
TIES: HUMANITIES SERIES, NO. 1:   Liedloff, Steinbeck in German Translation   121

THE NORTON LIBRARY: Bryer, ed., Sixteen Modern American
Authors   174

SCARECROW AUTHOR BIBLIOGRAPHIES, NO. 64:   Hayashi, A New
Steinbeck Bibliography, 1971-1981   88; see also 87

STEINBECK MONOGRAPH SERIES, NO. 1:   Hayashi, John Steinbeck:
A Guide to the Doctoral Dissertations   85; NO. 2:   Garcia, Stein-
beck and D. H. Lawrence   64; NO. 3:   Jones, John Steinbeck As
Fabulist   107; NO. 4:   Hayashi, ed., Steinbeck Criticism: A Re-
view of Book-Length Studies   182; NO. 5:   Hayashi, Steinbeck
and the Arthurian Theme   180; NO. 6:   Simmonds, Steinbeck's
Literary Achievement   171; NO. 7:   Ditsky, Essays on "East of
Eden"   48; NO. 8:   International Steinbeck Congress, 1st, Kyushu
University, 1976, Steinbeck, East and West   103; No. 9:   Hayashi,
ed., Steinbeck's Women   186; NO. 10:   Hayashi, ed., Steinbeck's
Travel Literature   185; NO. 11:   Hayashi, ed., A Handbook for
Steinbeck Collectors   70

STUDIES IN AMERICAN LITERATURE, V. 11:   Marks, Thematic Design in the Novels of John Steinbeck   130

TWAYNE'S UNITED STATES AUTHOR'S SERIES, TUSAS, 2:   French,
John Steinbeck   62

UNIVERSITY OF MINNESOTA PAMPHLETS ON AMERICAN WRITERS,
NO. 94:   Gray, John Steinbeck   68

THE VIKING CRITICAL LIBRARY: Lisca, ed., "Bibliography," IN
Steinbeck, J., The Grapes of Wrath, Text and Criticism   122

JOURNAL INDEX

Many bibliographies are contained in journal articles and are valuable to the researcher. A listing of those about John Steinbeck will be of use in locating items that would be difficult to find otherwise. Each journal title is listed alphabetically and those articles contained therein are arranged in the same order below. Linkage to the items contained in the bibliography is the same sequential numbering system employed in the other indexes in this part. In several of the periodicals related to John Steinbeck cited below, no specific bibliographical articles are listed because they include many articles of a bibliographical nature.

Bulletin of Bibliography: Steele, "John Steinbeck: A Checklist of Biographical, Critical, and Bibliographical Material" 178

Colophon (New Series): Powell, "Toward a Bibliography of John Steinbeck" 152

John Steinbeck Society of Japan Newsletter 105

Kyushu Amerika Bungaku (Kyushu American Literature): Hayashi, "Brief Survey of John Steinbeck Bibliographies" 78

Modern Fiction Studies: Beebe and Bryer, "Criticism of John Steinbeck" 14

Publishers Weekly: Powell, "John (Ernst) Steinbeck, 1902- " 151

San Jose Studies: Woodward, The Steinbeck Research Center at San Jose State University: A Descriptive Catalogue 200

Serif: Hayashi, "John Steinbeck: A Checklist of Movie Reviews" 81; Hayashi, "John Steinbeck: A Checklist of Unpublished Ph.D. Dissertations" 82

Steinbeck Collector 181

Steinbeck Newsletter (now Steinbeck Quarterly): Hayashi, "Checklist of Steinbeck Criticism After 1963" 79

Steinbeck Newsletter (India) 182a